180 Days of
PRACTICE

GRADE
K

HANDS-ON STEAM

Science | Technology | Engineering | Arts | Mathematics

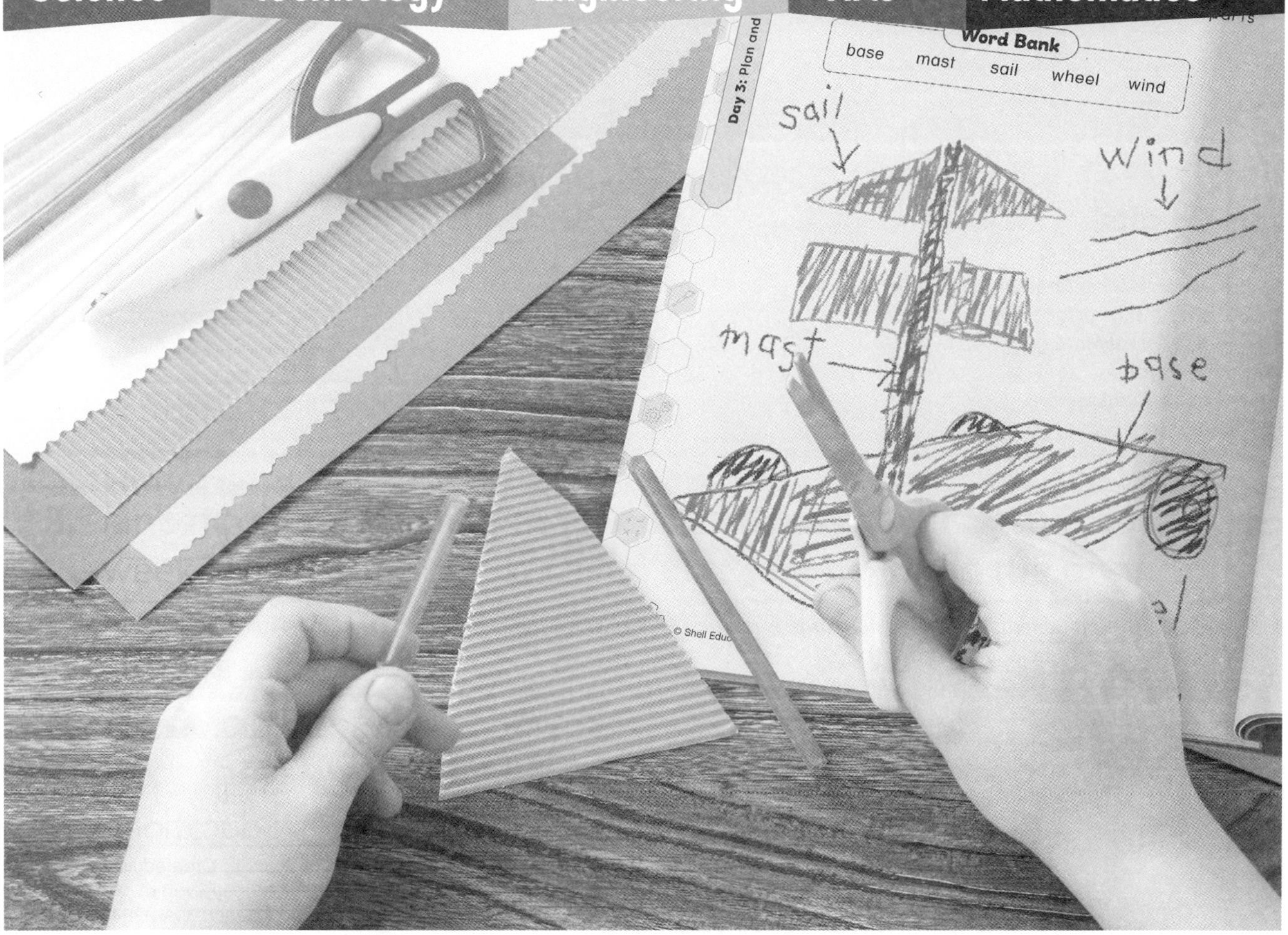

Chandra Prough, M.S.Ed., NBCT

Program Credits

Corinne Burton, M.A.Ed., *Publisher*
Emily R. Smith, M.A.Ed., *VP of Content Development*
Véronique Bos, *Creative Director*
Lynette Ordoñez, *Content Manager*
Melissa Laughlin, *Editor*
Jill Malcolm, *Graphic Designer*
David Slayton, *Assistant Editor*

Image Credits

pp. 51, 58, 60, 175 Jill Malcolm; all other images from iStock and/or Shutterstock

Standards

NGSS Lead States. 2013. *Next Generation Science Standards: For States, By States*. Washington, DC: The National Academies Press.
© 2021 TESOL International Association
© 2021 Board of Regents of the University of Wisconsin System

Shell Education
A division of Teacher Created Materials
5482 Argosy Avenue
Huntington Beach, CA 92649
www.tcmpub.com/shell-education
ISBN 978-1-4258-2527-0

Table of Contents

Introduction

Research 4
- The Importance of STEAM Education 4
- Defining STEAM 5
- The Engineering Design Process 6
- How to Facilitate Successful STEAM Challenges 7

How to Use This Resource 9
- Unit Structure Overview 9
- Pacing Options 10
- Teaching Support Pages 11
- Student Pages 12
- Assessment Options 14

Standards Correlations 15

180 Days of Practice

Physical Science

Unit 1: Objects in Motion 17
Unit 2: Properties of Matter 34
Unit 3: Pushes and Pulls 51

Life Science

Unit 4: Animal Homes 68
Unit 5: Living and Nonliving Things 85
Unit 6: The Five Senses 102
Unit 7: Plants 119

Earth Science

Unit 8: Earth's Resources 136
Unit 9: Reduce, Reuse, Recycle 153
Unit 10: Severe Weather 170
Unit 11: Warmth from the Sun 187
Unit 12: Wind 204

Appendixes

STEAM Challenge Rubric 221
Summative Assessment 222
Engineering Design Process 223
Digital Resources 224
References Cited 224

Research

The Importance of STEAM Education

STEAM education is a powerful approach to learning that continues to gain momentum and support across the globe. STEAM is the integration of science, technology, engineering, the arts, and mathematics to design solutions for real-world problems. Students must learn how to question, explore, and analyze natural phenomena. With these skills in hand, students understand the complexity of available information and are empowered to become independent learners and problem solvers.

The content and practices of STEAM education are strong components of a balanced instructional approach, ensuring students are college- and career-ready. The application of STEAM practices in the classroom affords teachers opportunities to challenge students to apply new knowledge. Students of all ages can design and build structures, improve existing products, and test innovative solutions to real-world problems. STEAM instruction can be as simple as using recycled materials to design a habitat for caterpillars discovered on the playground and as challenging as designing a solution to provide clean water to developing countries. The possibilities are endless.

Blending arts principles with STEM disciplines prepares students to be problem solvers, creative collaborators, and thoughtful risk-takers. Even students who do not choose a career in a STEAM field will benefit because these skills can be translated into almost any career. Students who become STEAM proficient are prepared to answer complex questions, investigate global issues, and develop solutions for real-world challenges. Roger W. Bybee (2013, 64) summarizes what is expected of students as they join the workforce:

> As literate adults, individuals should be competent to understand STEM-related global issues; recognize scientific from other nonscientific explanations; make reasonable arguments based on evidence; and, very important, fulfill their civic duties at the local, national, and global levels.

Likewise, STEAM helps students understand how concepts are connected as they gain proficiency in the Four Cs: creativity, collaboration, critical thinking, and communication.

Research *(cont.)*

Defining STEAM

STEAM is an integrated way of preparing students for the twenty-first century world. It places an emphasis on understanding science and mathematics while learning engineering skills. By including art, STEAM recognizes that the creative aspect of any project is integral to good design—whether designing an experiment or an object.

Science

Any project or advancement builds on prior science knowledge. Science focuses on learning and applying specific content, cross-cutting concepts, and scientific practices that are relevant to the topic or project.

Technology

This is what results from the application of scientific knowledge and engineering. It is something that is created to solve a problem or meet a need. Some people also include the *use* of technology in this category. That is, tools used by scientists and engineers to solve problems. In addition to computers and robots, technology can include nets used by marine biologists, anemometers used by meteorologists, computer software used by mathematicians, and so on.

Engineering

This is the application of scientific knowledge to meet a need, solve a problem, or address phenomena. For example, engineers design bridges to withstand huge loads. Engineering is also used to understand phenomena, such as in designing a way to test a hypothesis. When problems arise, such as those due to earthquakes or rising sea levels, engineering is required to design solutions to the problems. On a smaller scale, a homeowner might want to find a solution to their basement flooding.

Art

In this context, art equals creativity and creative problem-solving. For example, someone might want to test a hypothesis but be stumped as to how to set up the experiment. Perhaps you have a valuable painting. You think there is another valuable image below the first layer of paint on the canvas. You do not want to destroy the painting on top. A creative solution is needed. Art can also include a creative or beautiful design that solves a problem. For example, the Golden Gate Bridge is considered both an engineering marvel and a work of art.

Mathematics

This is the application of mathematics to real-world problems. Often, this includes data analysis—such as collecting data, graphing it, analyzing the data, and then communicating that analysis. It may also include taking mathematical measurements in the pursuit of an answer. The idea is not to learn new math, but rather to apply it; however, some mathematics may need to be learned to solve the specific problem. Isaac Newton, for example, is famous for *inventing* calculus to help him solve problems in understanding gravity and motion.

Research *(cont.)*

The Engineering Design Process

The most essential component of STEAM education is the engineering design process. This process is an articulated approach to problem solving in which students are guided through the iterative process of solving problems and refining solutions to achieve the best possible outcomes. There are many different versions of the engineering design process, but they all have the same basic structure and goals. As explained in Appendix I of NGSS (2013), "At any stage, a problem-solver can redefine the problem or generate new solutions to replace an idea that just isn't working out."

Each unit in this resource presents students with a design challenge in an authentic and engaging context. The practice pages guide and support students through the engineering design process to solve problems or fulfill needs.

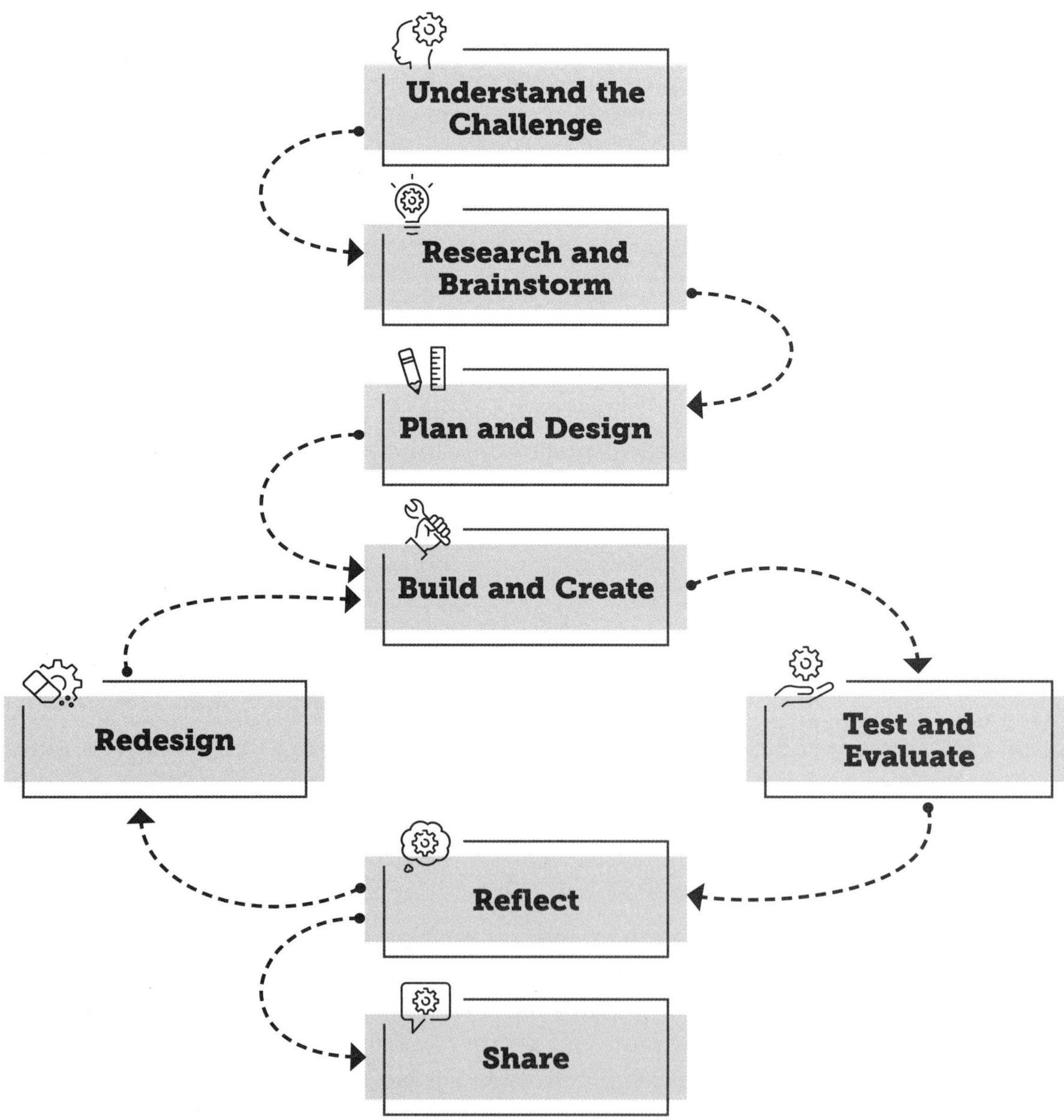

Research *(cont.)*

How to Facilitate Successful STEAM Challenges

There are some basic rules to remember as your students complete STEAM challenges.

Both independent and collaborative work should be included.

Astronaut and inventor Ellen Ochoa is well-known for working a robotic arm in space. About that experience she said, "It's fun to work the robotic arm, in part because it's a team effort." She recognized that she was getting credit for something amazing that happened because of the collaborative work of hundreds of people.

Students need time to think through a project, both on their own and together with others. It is often best to encourage students to start by thinking independently. One student may think of a totally different solution than another student. Once they come together, students can merge aspects of each other's ideas to devise something even better.

Failure is a step in the process.

During the process of trying to invent a useful light bulb, Thomas Edison famously said, "I have not failed. I've just found 10,000 ways that won't work." People are innovating when they are failing because it is a chance to try something new. The STEAM challenges in this book intentionally give students chances to improve their designs. Students should feel free to innovate as much as possible, especially the first time around. Then, they can build on what they learned and try again.

Some students get stuck thinking there is one right way. There are almost always multiple solutions to a problem. For example, attaching train cars together used to be very dangerous. In the late nineteenth century, different solutions to this problem were invented in England and the United States to make the process safer. Both solutions worked, and both were used! Encourage students to recognize that there are usually different ways to solve problems. Discuss the pros and cons of the various solutions that students generate.

Research *(cont.)*

How to Facilitate Successful STEAM Challenges *(cont.)*

Getting inspiration from others is an option.

Students worry a lot about copying. It is important to remind them that all breakthroughs come on the shoulders of others. No one is working in a vacuum, and it is okay to get inspiration and ideas from others. It is also important to give credit to the people whose work and ideas inspired others. Students may see this as cheating, but they should be encouraged to see that they had a great enough idea that others recognized it and wanted to build on it.

The struggle is real—and really important.

Most people do not like to fail. And it can be frustrating not to know what to do or what to try next. Lonnie Johnson, engineer and toy inventor, advises, "Persevere. That's what I always say to people. There's no easy route." Try to support students during this struggle, as amazing innovations can emerge from the process. Further, students feel great when they surprise themselves with success after thinking they were not going to succeed.

Materials can inspire the process.

Students may be stumped about how they are going to build a boat…until you show them that they can use clay. A parachute is daunting, but a pile of tissue paper or plastic bags might suddenly make students feel like they have some direction. On the other hand, materials can also instantly send the mind in certain directions, without exploring other options. For this reason, consider carefully the point at which you want to show students the materials they can use. You might want them to brainstorm materials first. This might inspire you to offer materials you had not considered before.

Some students or groups will need different types of support.

If possible, have students who need additional support manipulate materials, play with commercial solutions, or watch videos to get ideas. For students who need an additional challenge, consider ways to make the challenge more "real world" by adding additional realistic criteria. Or, encourage students to add their own criteria.

How to Use This Resource

Unit Structure Overview

This resource is organized into 12 units. Each three-week unit is organized in a consistent format for ease of use.

Week 1: STEAM Content

Day 1 **Learn Content**	Students read text, study visuals, and answer multiple-choice questions.
Day 2 **Learn Content**	Students read text, study visuals, and answer short-answer questions.
Day 3 **Explore Content**	Students engage in hands-on activities, such as scientific investigations, mini building challenges, and drawing and labeling diagrams.
Day 4 **Get Creative**	Students use their creativity, imaginations, and artistic abilities in activities such as drawing, creating fun designs, and doing science-related crafts.
Day 5 **Analyze Data**	Students analyze and/or create charts, tables, maps, and graphs.

Week 2: STEAM Challenge

Day 1 **Understand the Challenge**	Students are introduced to the STEAM Challenge. They review the criteria and constraints for successful designs.
Day 2 **Research and Brainstorm**	Students conduct additional research, as needed, and brainstorm ideas for their designs.
Day 3 **Plan and Design**	Students plan and sketch their designs.
Day 4 **Build and Create**	Students use their materials to construct their designs.
Day 5 **Test and Evaluate**	Students conduct tests and/or evaluation to assess the effectiveness of their designs and how well they met the criteria of the challenge.

Week 3: STEAM Challenge Improvement

Day 1 **Reflect**	Students answer questions to reflect on their first designs and make plans for how to improve their designs.
Day 2 **Redesign**	Students sketch new or modified designs.
Day 3 **Rebuild and Refine**	Students rebuild or adjust their designs.
Day 4 **Retest**	Students retest and evaluate their new designs.
Day 5 **Reflect and Share**	Students reflect on their experiences working through the engineering design process. They discuss and share their process and results with others.

How to Use This Resource *(cont.)*

Pacing Options

This resource is flexibly designed and can be used in tandem with a core curriculum within a science, STEAM, or STEM block. It can also be used in makerspaces, after-school programs, summer school, or as enrichment activities at home. The following pacing options show suggestions for how to use this book.

Option 1

This option shows how each unit can be completed in 15 days. This option requires approximately 10–20 minutes per day. Building days are flexible, and teachers may allow for additional time at their discretion.

	Day 1	Day 2	Day 3	Day 4	Day 5
Week 1	Learn Content	Learn Content	Explore Content	Get Creative	Analyze Data
Week 2	Understand the Challenge	Research and Brainstorm	Plan and Design	Build and Create	Test and Evaluate
Week 3	Reflect	Redesign	Rebuild and Refine	Retest	Reflect and Share

Option 2

This option shows how each unit can be completed in fewer than 15 days. This option requires approximately 45–60 minutes a day.

	Day 1	Day 2
Week 1	Learn Content Explore Content	Get Creative Analyze Data
Week 2	Understand the Challenge Research and Brainstorm Plan and Design	Build and Create Test and Evaluate
Week 3	Reflect Redesign Rebuild and Refine	Retest Reflect and Share

How to Use This Resource *(cont.)*

Teaching Support Pages

Each unit in this resource begins with two teaching support pages that provide instructional guidance.

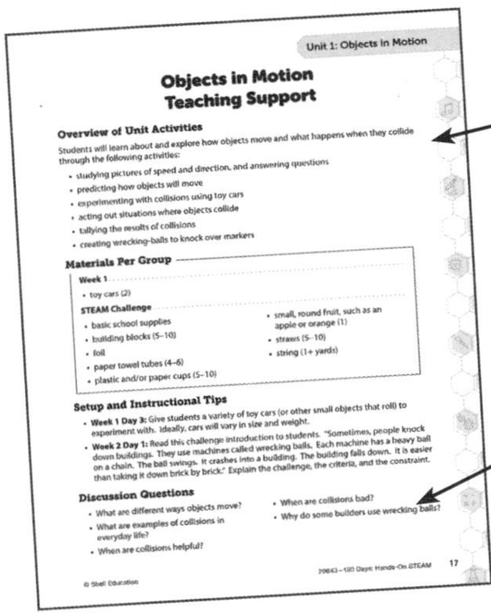

Unit 1: Objects in Motion

Objects in Motion Teaching Support

Overview of Unit Activities

Students will learn about and explore how objects move and what happens when they collide through the following activities:

- studying pictures of speed and direction, and answering questions
- predicting how objects will move
- experimenting with collisions using toy cars
- acting out situations where objects collide
- tallying the results of collisions
- creating wrecking-balls to knock over markers

Materials Per Group

Week 1

- toy cars (2)

STEAM Challenge

- basic school supplies
- building blocks (5–10)
- foil
- paper towel tubes (4–6)
- plastic and/or paper cups (5–10)
- small, round fruit, such as an apple or orange (1)
- straws (5–10)
- string (1+ yards)

Setup and Instructional Tips

- **Week 1 Day 3:** Give students a variety of toy cars (or other small objects that roll) to experiment with. Ideally, cars will vary in size and weight.
- **Week 2 Day 1:** Read this challenge introduction to students. "Sometimes, people knock down buildings. They use machines called wrecking balls. Each machine has a heavy ball on a chain. The ball swings. It crashes into a building. The building falls down. It is easier than taking it down brick by brick." Explain the challenge, the criteria, and the constraint.

Discussion Questions

- What are different ways objects move?
- What are examples of collisions in everyday life?
- When are collisions helpful?
- When are collisions bad?
- Why do some builders use wrecking balls?

© Shell Education 29643—180 Days: Hands-On STEAM 17

A clear overview of unit activities, weekly materials, safety notes, and setup tips helps teachers plan and prepare efficiently and with ease.

Discussion questions encourage students to verbalize their learning and connect it to their own lives.

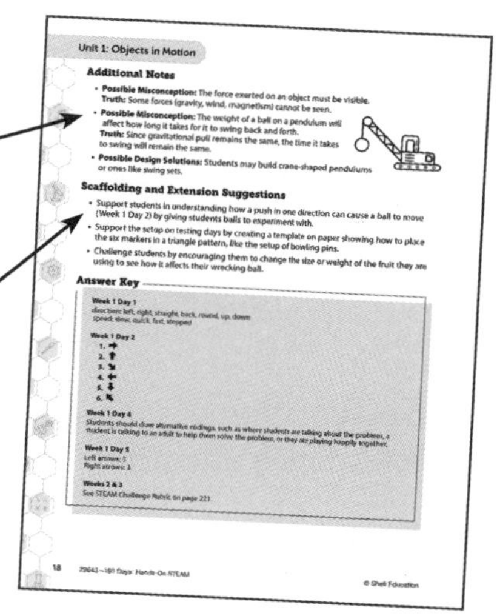

Unit 1: Objects in Motion

Additional Notes

- **Possible Misconception:** The force exerted on an object must be visible.
  Truth: Some forces (gravity, wind, magnetism) cannot be seen.
- **Possible Misconception:** The weight of a ball on a pendulum will affect how long it takes for it to swing back and forth.
  Truth: Since gravitational pull remains the same, the time it takes to swing will remain the same.
- **Possible Design Solutions:** Students may build crane-shaped pendulums or ones like swing sets.

Scaffolding and Extension Suggestions

- Support students in understanding how a push in one direction can cause a ball to move (Week 1 Day 2) by giving students balls to experiment with.
- Support the setup on testing days by creating a template on paper showing how to place the six markers in a triangle pattern, like the setup of bowling pins.
- Challenge students by encouraging them to change the size or weight of the fruit they are using to see how it affects their wrecking ball.

Answer Key

Week 1 Day 1
direction: left, right, straight, back, round, up, down
speed: slow, quick, fast, stopped

Week 1 Day 2
1. →
2. ↑
3. ↘
4. ←
5. ↓
6. ↖

Week 1 Day 4
Students should draw alternative endings, such as where students are talking about the problem, a student is talking to an adult to help them solve the problem, or they are playing happily together.

Week 1 Day 5
Left arrows: 5
Right arrows: 3

Weeks 2 & 3
See STEAM Challenge Rubric on page 221.

18 29643—180 Days: Hands-On STEAM © Shell Education

Possible student misconceptions and design solutions further take the guesswork out of lesson planning.

Differentiation options offer ways to support and extend student learning.

Materials

Due to the nature of engineering, the materials listed are often flexible. They may be substituted or added to, depending on what you have available. More material options require greater consideration by students and encourage more creative and critical thinking. Fewer material options can help narrow students' focus but may limit creativity. Adjust the materials provided to fit the needs of your students.

Approximate amounts of materials are included in each list. These amount suggestions are per group. Students are expected to have basic school supplies for each unit. These include paper, pencils, markers or crayons, glue, tape, and scissors.

How to Use This Resource *(cont.)*

Student Pages

Be sure to read aloud all text on student pages, and support comprehension as needed. At this level, students may need additional support brainstorming or designing solutions for the STEAM Challenges. See the differentiation suggestions on the Teaching Support Pages for additional ways to support students.

Students begin each unit by learning about and exploring science-related content.

Activities in **Week 1** help build background science content knowledge relevant to the STEAM Challenge.

Creative activities encourage students to connect science and art.

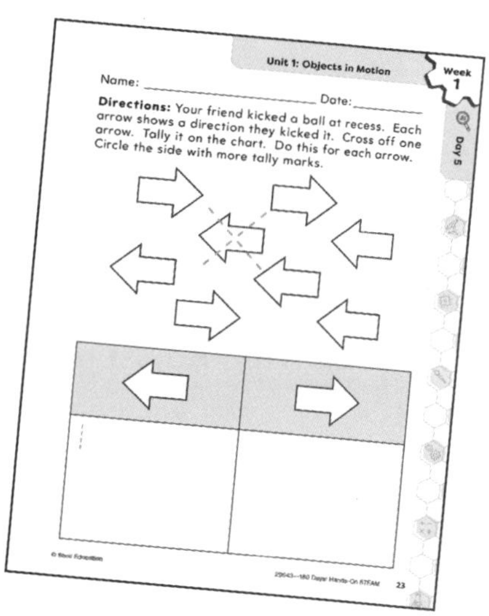

Graphs, charts, and maps guide students to make important mathematics and real-world connections

How to Use This Resource *(cont.)*

Student Pages *(cont.)*

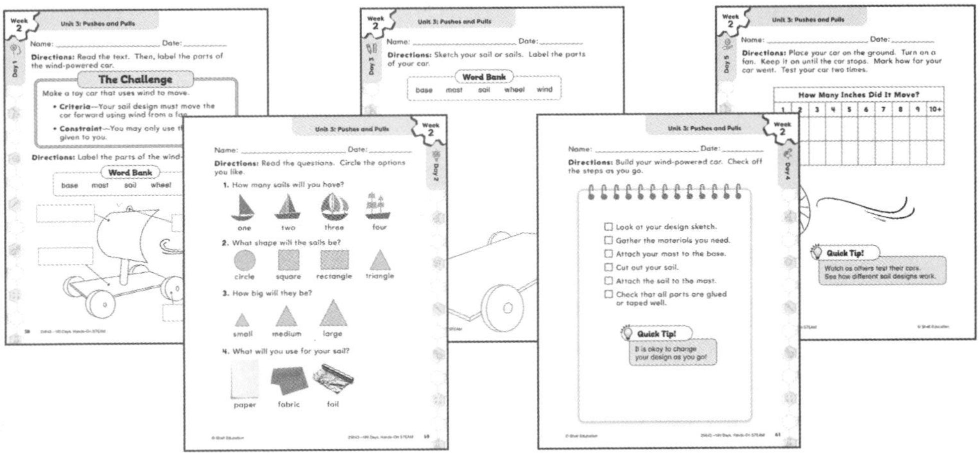

Week 2 introduces students to the STEAM Challenge. Activities guide students through each step of the engineering design process. They provide guiding questions and space for students to record their plans, progress, results, and thinking.

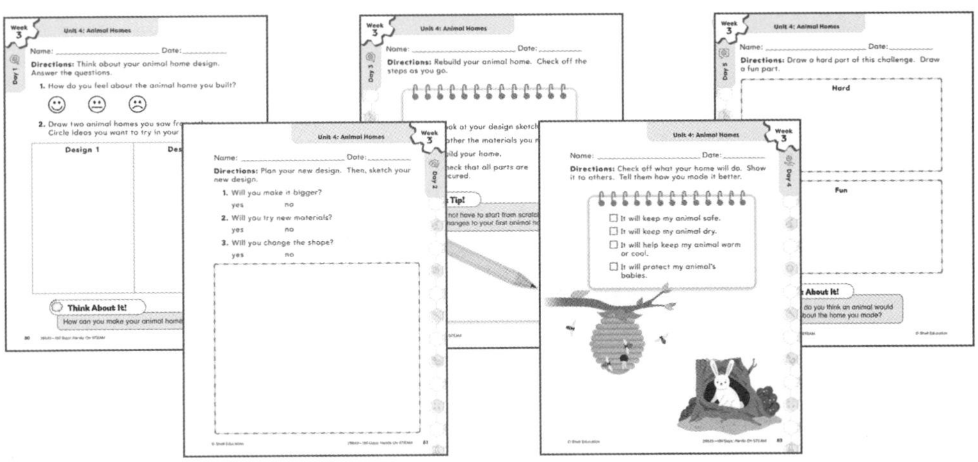

Week 3 activities continue to lead students through the cycle of the engineering design process. Students are encouraged to think about and discuss ways to improve their designs based on their observations and experiences in Week 2.

Quick Tip!

Staple all the student pages for each unit together, and distribute them as packets. This will allow students to easily refer to their learning as they complete the STEAM Challenges.

How to Use This Resource *(cont.)*

Assessment Options

Assessments guide instructional decisions and improve student learning. This resource offers balanced assessment opportunities. The assessments require students to think critically, respond to text-dependent questions, and utilize science and engineering practices.

Progress Monitoring

There are key points throughout each unit when valuable formative evaluations can be made. These evaluations can be based on group, paired, and/or individual discussions and activities.

- **Week 1** activities provide opportunities for students to answer multiple-choice and short-answer questions related to the content. Answer keys for these pages are provided in the Teaching Support pages.

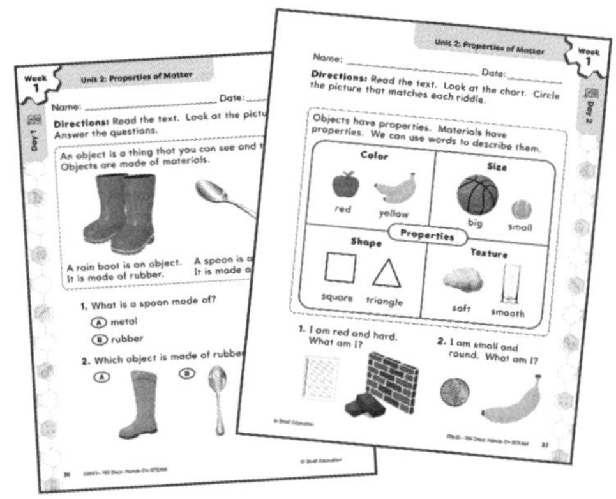

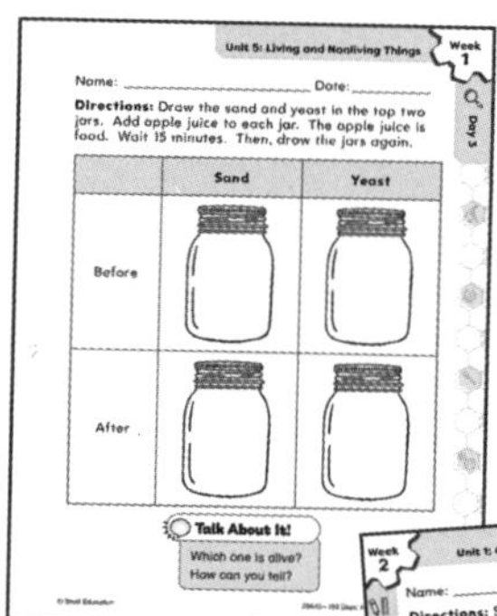

- **Talk About It!** graphics on student activity sheets offer opportunities to monitor student progress.

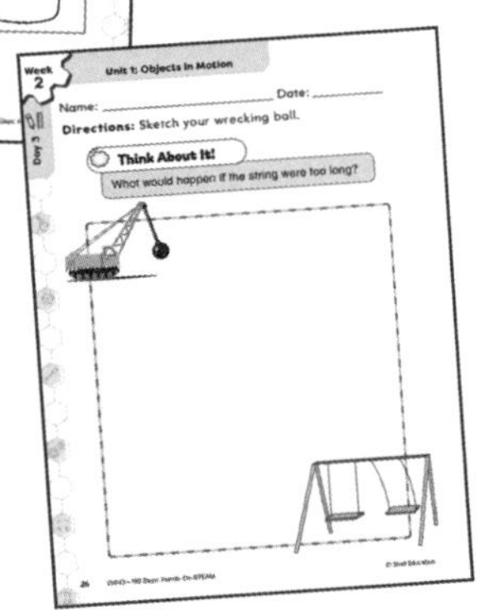

- **Week 2 Day 3: Plan and Design** is when students sketch their first designs. This is a great opportunity to assess how well students understand the STEAM challenge and what they plan to create. These should be reviewed before moving on to the Build and Create stages of the STEAM Challenges.

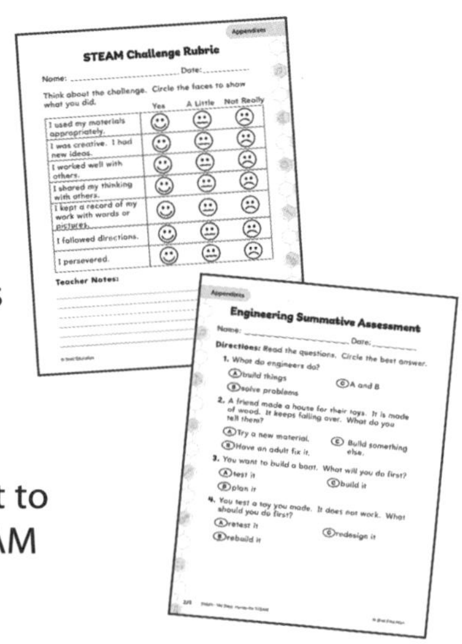

Summative Assessment

A rubric for the STEAM Challenges is provided on page 221. It is important to note that whether students' final designs were successful is not the main goal of this assessment. It is a way to assess students' skills as they work through the engineering design process. Students assess themselves first. Teachers can add notes to the assessment.

A short summative assessment is provided on page 222. This is meant to provide teachers with insight into how well students understand STEAM practices and the engineering design process.

Standards Correlations

Shell Education is committed to producing educational materials that are research and standards based. To support this effort, this resource is correlated to the academic standards of all 50 states, the District of Columbia, the Department of Defense Dependent Schools, and the Canadian provinces. A correlation is also provided for key professional educational organizations.

To print a customized correlation report for your state, visit our website at **www.tcmpub.com/administrators/correlations** and follow the online directions. If you require assistance in printing correlation reports, please contact the Customer Service Department at 1-800-858-7339.

Standards Overview

The Every Student Succeeds Act (ESSA) mandates that all states adopt challenging academic standards that help students meet the goal of college and career readiness. While many states already adopted academic standards prior to ESSA, the act continues to hold states accountable for detailed and comprehensive standards. Standards are designed to focus instruction and guide adoption of curricula. They define the knowledge, skills, and content students should acquire at each level. Standards are also used to develop standardized tests to evaluate students' academic progress. State standards are used in the development of our resources, so educators can be assured they meet state academic requirements.

Next Generation Science Standards

This set of national standards aims to incorporate science knowledge and process standards into a cohesive framework. The standards listed on page 16 describe the science content and processes presented throughout the lessons.

TESOL and WIDA Standards

In this book, the following English language development standards are met: Standard 1: English language learners communicate for social and instructional purposes within the school setting. Standard 3: English language learners communicate information, ideas and concepts necessary for academic success in the content area of mathematics. Standard 4: English language learners communicate information, ideas and concepts necessary for academic success in the content area of science.

Standards Correlations *(cont.)*

Each unit in this resource supports the following NGSS Scientific and Engineering Practices and Engineering Performance Expectations for K–2.

Scientific and Engineering Practices	Engineering Performance Expectations
Asking Questions and Defining Problems	Ask questions, make observations, and gather information about a situation people want to change to define a simple problem that can be solved through the development of a new or improved object or tool.
Developing and Using Models	
Planning and Carrying Out Investigations	
Analyzing and Interpreting Data	Develop a simple sketch, drawing, or physical model to illustrate how the shape of an object helps it function as needed to solve a given problem.
Constructing Explanations and Designing Solutions	
Engaging in Argument from Evidence	Analyze data from tests of two objects designed to solve the same problem to compare the strengths and weaknesses of how each performs.
Obtaining, Evaluating, and Communicating Information	

This chart shows how the units in this resource align to NGSS Disciplinary Core Ideas and Crosscutting Concepts.

Unit	Disciplinary Core Idea	Crosscutting Concept
Objects in Motion	PS2.A: Forces and Motion PS3.C: Relationship Between Energy and Forces	Cause and Effect
Properties of Matter	PS1.A: Structures and Properties of Matter	Patterns; Energy and Matter
Pushes and Pulls	PS2.A: Forces and Motion PS2.B: Types of Interactions PS3.C: Relationship Between Energy and Forces	Cause and Effect
Animal Homes	ESS2.E: Biogeology	Patterns; Systems and System Models
Living and Nonliving Things	LS1.C: Org. of Matter and Energy Flow in Organisms	Patterns
The Five Senses	LS1.D: Informations Processing PS4.A: Wave Properties	Structure and Function
Plants	LS1.C: Org. of Matter and Energy Flow in Organisms	Patterns; Structure and Function
Earth's Resources	ESS3.A: Natural Resources	Cause and Effect; Systems and System Models
Reduce, Reuse, Recycle	ESS3.C: Human Impacts on Earth Systems	Patterns; Systems and System Models
Severe Weather	ESS3.B: Natural Hazards	Cause and Effect; Systems and System Models
Warmth from the Sun	PS3.B: Conservation of Energy and Energy Transfer	Cause and Effect
Wind	ESS2.D: Weather and Climate	Cause and Effect; Systems and System Models

Objects in Motion Teaching Support

Overview of Unit Activities

Students will learn about and explore how objects move and what happens when they collide through the following activities:

- studying pictures of speed and direction, and answering questions
- predicting how objects will move
- experimenting with collisions using toy cars
- acting out situations where objects collide
- tallying the results of collisions
- creating wrecking-balls to knock over markers

Materials Per Group

Week 1

- toy cars (2)

STEAM Challenge

- basic school supplies
- building blocks (5–10)
- foil
- paper towel tubes (4–6)
- plastic and/or paper cups (5–10)
- small, round fruit, such as an apple or orange (1)
- straws (5–10)
- string (1+ yards, 1+ meters)

Setup and Instructional Tips

- **Week 1 Day 3:** Give students a variety of toy cars (or other small objects that roll) to experiment with. Ideally, cars will vary in size and weight.
- **Week 2 Day 1:** Read this challenge introduction to students. "Sometimes, people knock down buildings. They use machines called wrecking balls. Each machine has a heavy ball on a chain. The ball swings. It crashes into a building. The building falls down. It is easier than taking it down brick by brick." Explain the challenge, the criteria, and the constraint.

Discussion Questions

- What are different ways objects move?
- What are examples of collisions in everyday life?
- When are collisions helpful?
- When are collisions bad?
- Why do some builders use wrecking balls?

Additional Notes

- **Possible Misconception:** The force exerted on an object must be visible.
  Truth: Some forces (gravity, wind, magnetism) cannot be seen.
- **Possible Misconception:** The weight of a ball on a pendulum will affect how long it takes for it to swing back and forth.
  Truth: Since gravitational pull remains the same, the time it takes to swing will remain the same.
- **Possible Design Solutions:** Students may build crane-shaped pendulums or ones like swing sets.

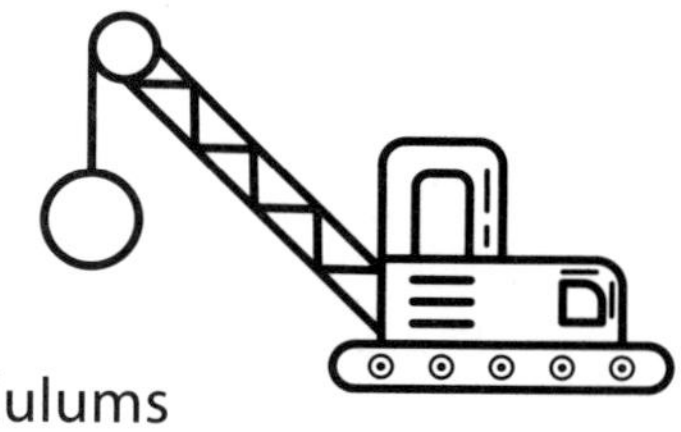

Scaffolding and Extension Suggestions

- Support students in understanding how a push in one direction can cause a ball to move (Week 1 Day 2) by giving students balls to experiment with.
- Support the setup on testing days by creating a template on paper showing how to place the six markers in a triangle pattern, like the setup of bowling pins.
- Challenge students by encouraging them to change the size or weight of the fruits they are using to see how it affects their wrecking balls.

Answer Key

Week 1 Day 1
direction: left, right, straight, back, round, up, down
speed: slow, quick, fast, stopped

Week 1 Day 2
1. ➡
2. ⬆
3. ↘
4. ⬅
5. ⬇
6. ↖

Week 1 Day 4
Students should draw alternative endings, such as where students are talking about the problem, a student is talking to an adult to help them solve the problem, or they are playing happily together.

Week 1 Day 5
Left arrows: 5
Right arrows: 3
The left side should be circled.

Weeks 2 & 3
See STEAM Challenge Rubric on page 221.

Name: ______________________________ Date: ____________

Directions: Read the text. Look at the pictures. Then, draw a line to match each word on the left to a word on the right.

Objects move at different speeds. Objects move in different directions.

speed

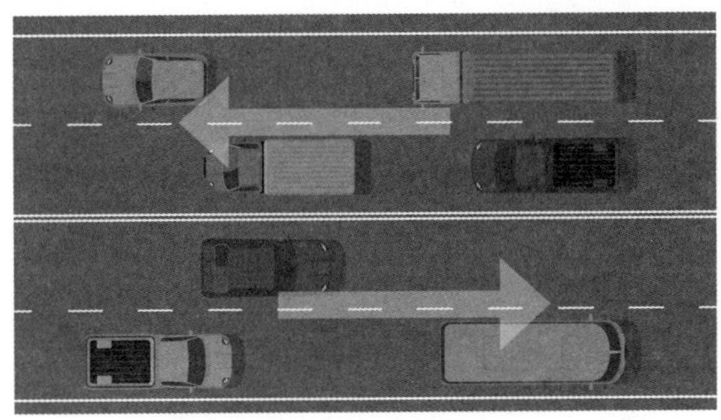

direction

left	
slow	
quick	
right	**speed**
straight	
fast	
stopped	**direction**
back	
up	
down	

Name: ______________________ Date: ____________

Directions: You can push things in different directions. Look at the person moving each ball. Draw an arrow to show which way the ball will move.

1.

4.

2.

5.

3.

6.

Name: ______________________ Date: __________

Directions: Read the text. Look at the pictures. Then, make two toy cars collide. Try it from different directions. Try it fast and slow. Draw pictures to show what happened.

When objects bump into each other, they collide. They can change speed. They can change direction.

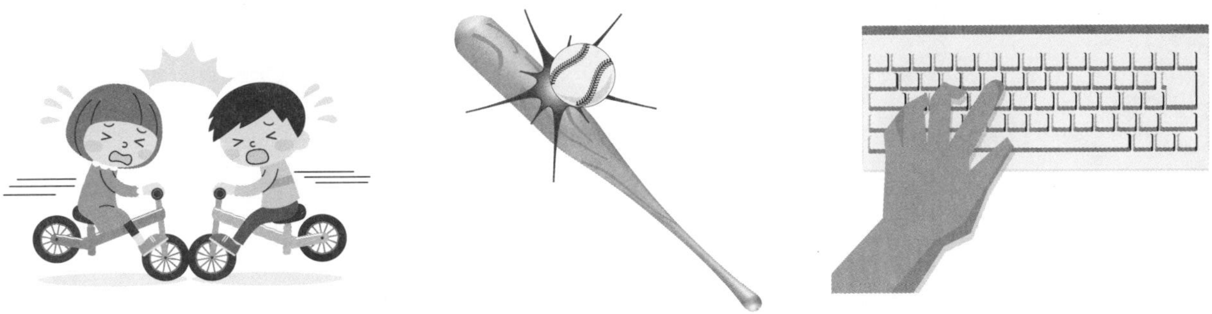

My Car Collision Observations

Day 4

Name: ______________________________ Date: ____________

Directions: Some collisions are accidents. Look at the story. Can you think of a better ending? Act it out with a friend. Then, draw a way both kids can feel better.

Story

My New Ending

Name: ______________________ Date: __________

Directions: Your friend kicked a ball at recess. Each arrow shows a direction they kicked it. Cross off one arrow. Tally it on the chart. Do this for each arrow. Circle the side with more tally marks.

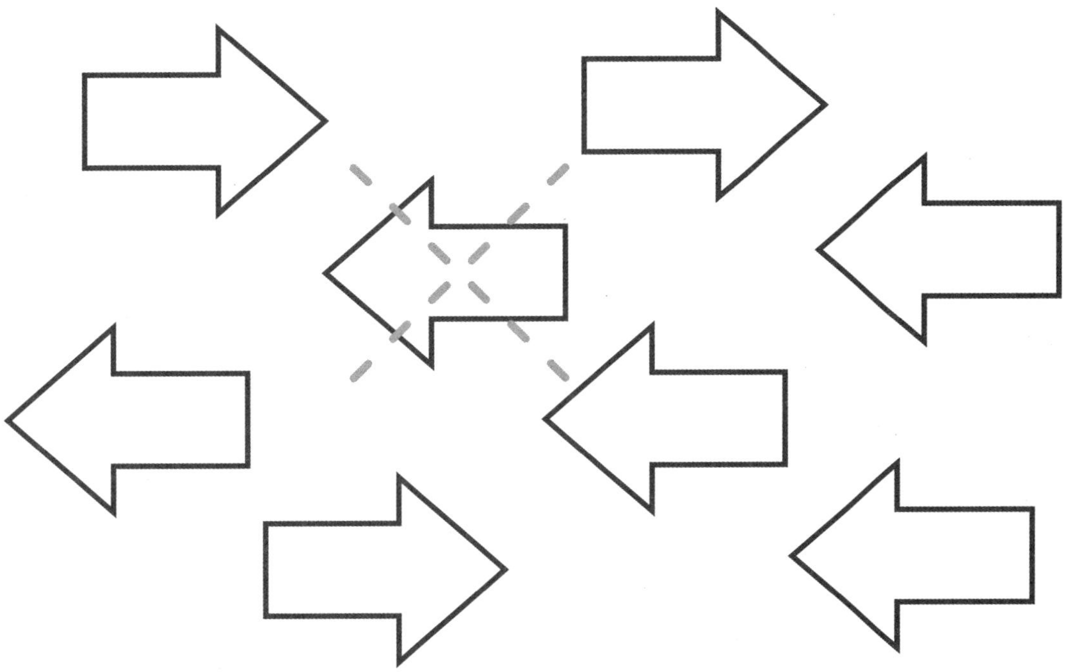

Name: ______________________________ Date: ____________

Directions: Read the text. Then, look at the picture. Circle the part that swings.

The Challenge

Make a toy wrecking ball.

- **Criteria**—Your wrecking ball must knock down six markers.
- **Constraint**—Use a piece of fruit for the ball.

Name: ______________________ Date: ____________

Directions: Read the text. Look at the picture. Then, answer the questions.

Wrecking Ball Research

A wrecking ball has a ball that swings. A short string makes it swing faster. The ball does not move as far. A long string makes it swing slower. The ball moves farther.

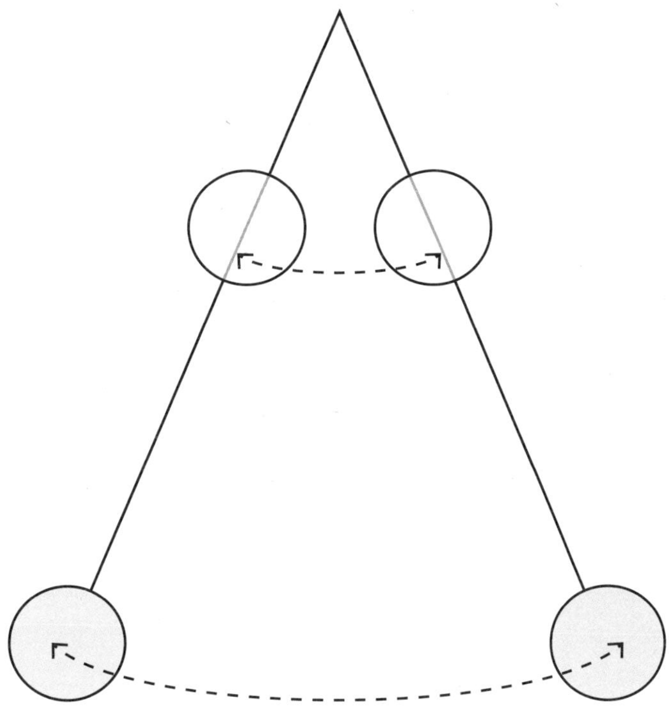

1. Do you want your pendulum to be **short** or **long**?

____

2. Why? Tell a partner.

Name: ______________________________ Date: ____________

Directions: Sketch your wrecking ball.

Think About It!

What would happen if the string were too long?

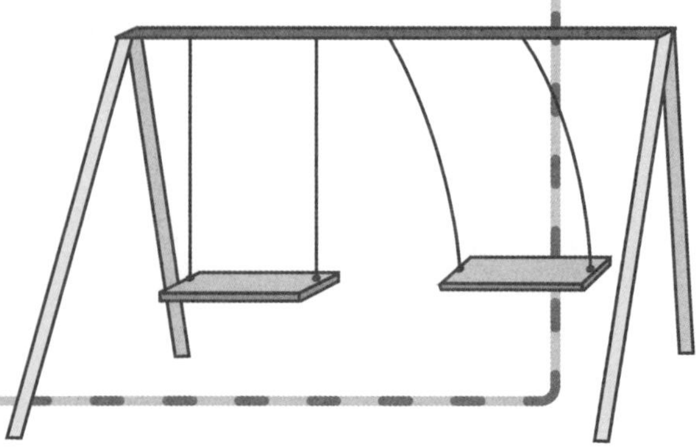

Name: ______________________________ Date: ____________

Directions: Build your wrecking ball. Check off the steps as you go.

- [ ] Look at your design sketch.
- [ ] Gather the materials you need.
- [ ] Build a frame for your wrecking ball. Make it sturdy.
- [ ] Cut and attach your string.
- [ ] Attach the fruit.
- [ ] Check that all parts are glued or taped well.
- [ ] Swing your fruit a few times. Make sure it works the way you want it to.

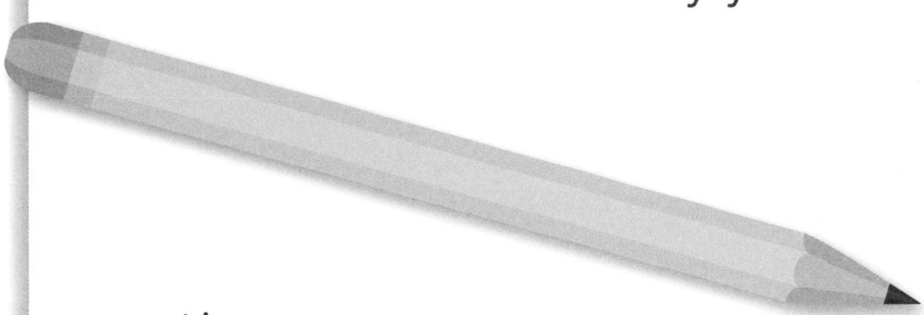

Quick Tip!

If you are stuck, look at what others are doing. Get ideas from them!

Name: ______________________________ Date: ____________

Directions: Place six markers in a triangle. Place your wrecking ball next them. Swing your wrecking ball. Record the results. Test it two more times.

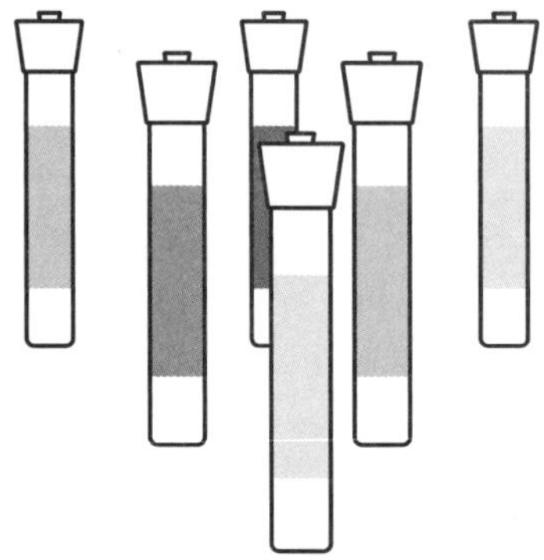

Test	Number of Markers Knocked Over
1	
2	
3	

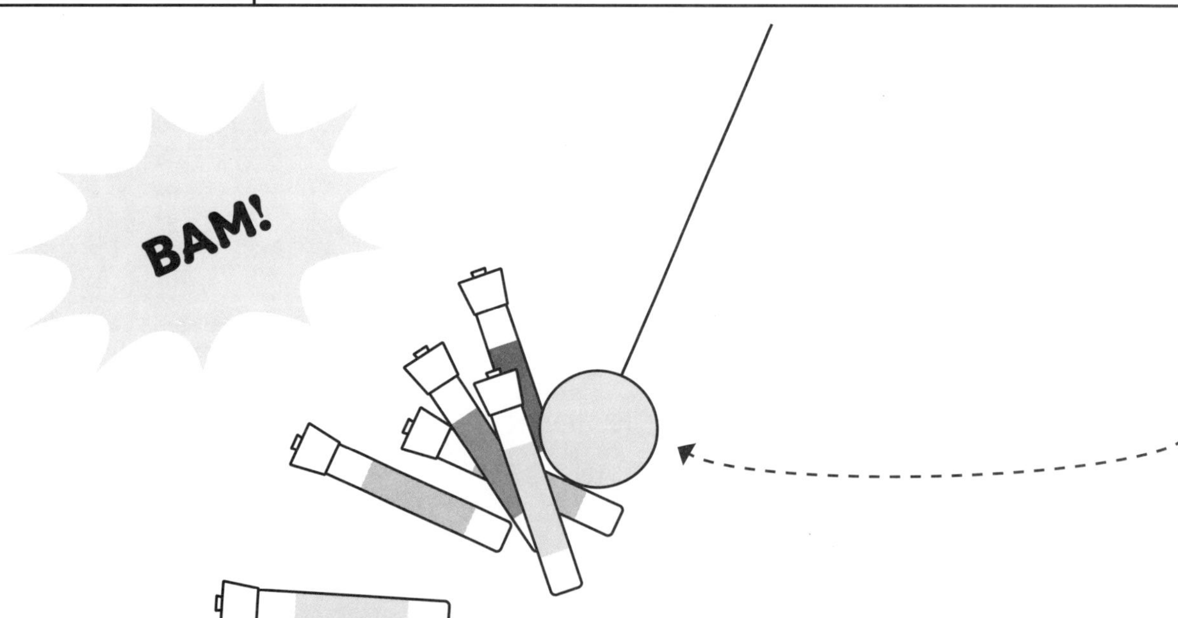

Name: ______________________________ Date: ____________

Directions: Think about your wrecking ball design. Answer the questions.

1. Look back at your tests. Circle the highest number of markers you knocked down in one test.

0 1 2 3 4 5 6

2. Draw two wrecking balls you saw from other groups. Put a checkmark by your favorite.

Design 1	Design 2

Try This!

Did your first design work well? If yes, plan to knock over more markers! How many will you try for?

Name: ______________________ Date: __________

Directions: Plan your new design. Then, sketch your new design.

1. Will you change the type of fruit you used? **yes** **no**
2. Will you change the frame of your wrecking ball? **yes** **no**
3. Will you change the length of your string? **yes** **no**
4. Will you change or add materials? **yes** **no**

Name: ______________________________ Date: ____________

Directions: Rebuild your wrecking ball. Make it work better. Use this list to help you.

- ☐ Look at your first design.
- ☐ Look at your plan to make it better.
- ☐ Get the materials you need.
- ☐ Take off parts you do not want.
- ☐ Add or make the changes you do want.
- ☐ Check that everything is glued or taped well.
- ☐ Swing your fruit a few times. Make sure it works the way you want it to.

Name: ______________________________ Date: ____________

Directions: Place your markers in a triangle. Place your wrecking ball next them. Test your wrecking ball. Record the results. Test it two more times.

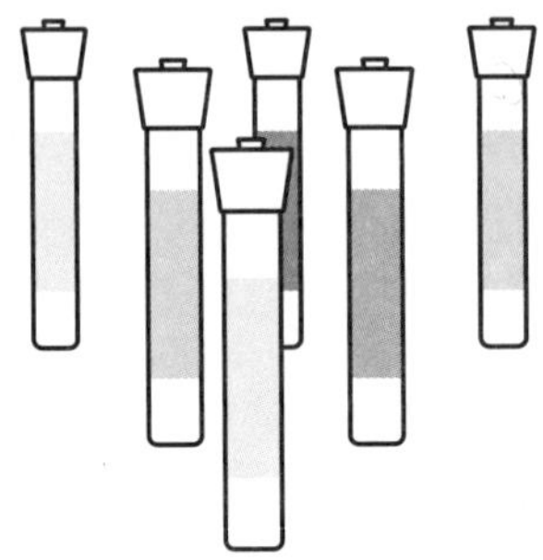

Test	Number of Markers Knocked Over
1	
2	
3	

Did your new wrecking ball knock over more markers?

yes **no**

Name: ______________________ Date: __________

Directions: Draw yourself as an engineer. Show your favorite part of this challenge.

Talk About It!

How did you solve a problem during this challenge?

Properties of Matter Teaching Support

Overview of Unit Activities

Students will learn about and explore properties of objects and materials through the following activities:

- learning about the properties of matter and answering questions
- solving riddles about objects based on their properties
- searching for objects with certain properties
- changing the properties of paper
- studying a chart of towers around the world
- building towers as tall as possible

Materials Per Group

Week 1

- basic school supplies

STEAM Challenge

- buttons (8)
- modeling clay (homemade option: 1 part baby lotion to two parts cornstarch)
- straws, cut into thirds (5)

Setup and Instructional Tips

- **Week 1 Day 4:** Give students construction paper and scissors. Review the properties of matter they can change (shape, size, texture).
- **Week 2 Day 1:** Read this challenge introduction to students. "There are many famous towers around the world. All of them are taller than they are wide. Towers are made from different objects and materials. You will make your tower out of buttons and modeling clay. Make it as tall as you can." Explain the challenge, the criteria, and the constraint.
- **Week 2 Day 4:** Give students buttons and modeling clay (no straws).
- **Week 3 Day 2:** Tell students that for their redesign they will also be able to use short straws.
- **Testing Days:** If using metric measurements, you may wish to recreate the charts on pages 45 and 49 to include higher values.

Discussion Questions

- What are some physical characteristics you can observe?
- What are some physical characteristics you can measure?
- How can things change over time?
- Look at a picture of a city skyline. What towers can you find?
- Where do you see towers at school or home?

Additional Notes

- **Possible Misconception:** All physical changes are irreversible.
  Truth: Some physical changes are reversable, such as melting ice, blowing up a balloon, crumping a sheet of paper, and stretching a rubber band.
- **Possible Design Solutions:** Students may shape the modeling clay into balls or disks; students may lay the buttons on their sides or stand them upright.
- **Materials:** Unless covered in plastic or placed in plastic bags, the modeling clay will harden overnight. Depending on your pacing plan, you may need to consider safely storing students' towers so that they do not harden and break.

Scaffolding and Extension Suggestions

- Support students with building tall towers by discussing how to maximize the materials (i.e., placing the buttons vertically rather than stacking them.)
- Challenge students by encouraging them to discuss the crosscutting concept of stability and change by observing the changes over time to the tower materials. Ask, "How did the clay change? Have the buttons changed? Would this affect how you build your tower if you wanted it to last one hour? One day? One week?"

Answer Key

Week 1 Day 1

1. A
2. A

Week 1 Day 2

1. a wall
2. a coin

Week 1 Day 3

Charts should have words or pictures that match each property, based on what students found.

Week 1 Day 5

1. B
2. A

Weeks 2 & 3

See STEAM Challenge Rubric on page 221.

Name: ______________________ Date: ____________

Directions: Read the text. Look at the pictures. Answer the questions.

An object is a thing that you can see and touch. Objects are made of materials.

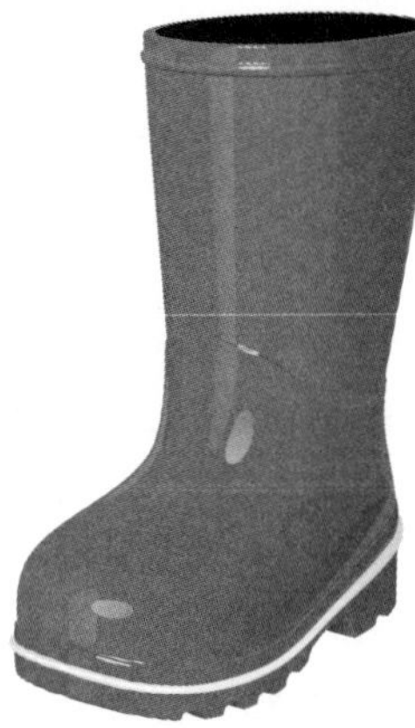

A rain boot is an object. It is made of rubber.

A spoon is an object. It is made of metal.

1. What is a spoon made of?

   (A) metal

   (B) rubber

2. Which object is made of rubber?

   (A) 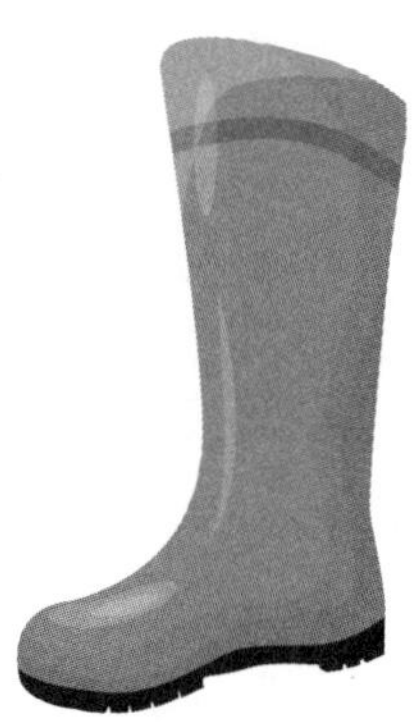

   (B) 

Name: ______________________________ Date: ____________

Directions: Read the text. Look at the chart. Circle the picture that matches each riddle.

Objects have properties. Materials have properties. We can use words to describe them.

Properties

Color

red

yellow

Size

big

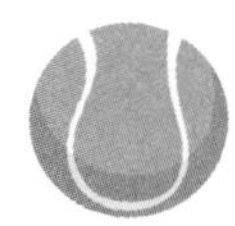
small

Shape

square

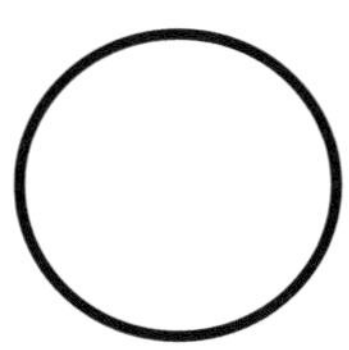
circle

Texture

soft

smooth

1. I am red and big. What am I?

2. I am small and a circle shape. What am I?

Name: ______________________ Date: ____________

Directions: Go on a scavenger hunt. Read each property in the chart. Find an object with that property. Write or draw it in the chart.

Property	Objects I Found
orange	
small	
bumpy	
round	
squishy	
tall	

Name: ______________________________ Date: ____________

Directions: Change the size and shape of two sheets of paper. Draw what they look like after.

Before	After

Name: ______________________ Date: __________

Directions: Towers are special buildings. They are taller than they are wide. Look at the chart. Answer the questions.

Towers Around the World				
Region	North America	Europe	Australia	South America
Tower				
Material	concrete	wood	stone	steel

1. Where is the tower made of wood?

Ⓐ North America Ⓑ Europe

2. Towers are very __________.

Ⓐ tall Ⓑ wide

Name: ______________________ Date: ____________

Directions: Read the text. Then, circle the tower.

The Challenge

A tower is a building that is taller than it is wide. Build a tower as tall as you can.

- **Criteria**—Your tower must stay standing.
- **Constraint**—Use 8 buttons and clay.

Name: ______________________ Date: __________

Directions: Read the text. Look at the pictures. Answer the question.

Towers have been built in different shapes and sizes. Towers must be stable. They must not fall over. This is not easy. The pictures show some shapes towers can have.

A	B	C

1. Which tower shape do you want to build?

A **B** **C**

Name: ______________________________ Date: ____________

Directions: Sketch your tower design. Label the parts.

Tower Parts

buttons clay top bottom

Name: ______________________ Date: __________

Directions: Build your tower. Check off the steps as you go.

- ☐ Look at your design sketch.
- ☐ Gather the materials: 8 buttons and some modeling clay.
- ☐ Build the tallest tower you can.
- ☐ Check to make sure you built a tower. Is it taller than it is wide?
- ☐ Gently push your tower to make sure it is stable.

Think About It!

How close does your tower look to your design sketch?

Name: ______________________________ Date: ____________

Directions: Measure your tower. Color the chart to record its height. Record the height of two other towers. Answer the question.

10			
9			
8			
7			
6			
5			
4			
3			
2			
1			
Height (in inches)	**Your Tower**	**Tower 2**	**Tower 3**

1. Which tower is the tallest?

Your Tower **Tower 2** **Tower 3**

Name: ______________________ Date: ____________

Directions: Think about your tower design. Answer the questions.

1. Were you happy with the height of your tower?

2. Draw two tower designs that you saw from other groups. Put a checkmark by the tallest one.

☐ **Design 1**	☐ **Design 2**

Talk About It!

What other materials would you want to use to build your tower?

Name: ______________________ Date: __________

Directions: You can now use straws to build your tower. Sketch your new tower design. Label the parts.

Tower Parts

buttons   clay   straws   top   bottom

Think About It!

Where will the straws work best?

Name: ______________________________ Date: ____________

Directions: Rebuild your tower. Make it taller. Check off the steps as you go.

- [ ] Look at your design sketch.
- [ ] Gather the materials: 8 buttons, 5 straws, and some modeling clay.
- [ ] Build the tallest tower you can.
- [ ] Check to make sure you built a tower. Is it taller than it is wide?
- [ ] Gently push your tower to make sure it is stable.

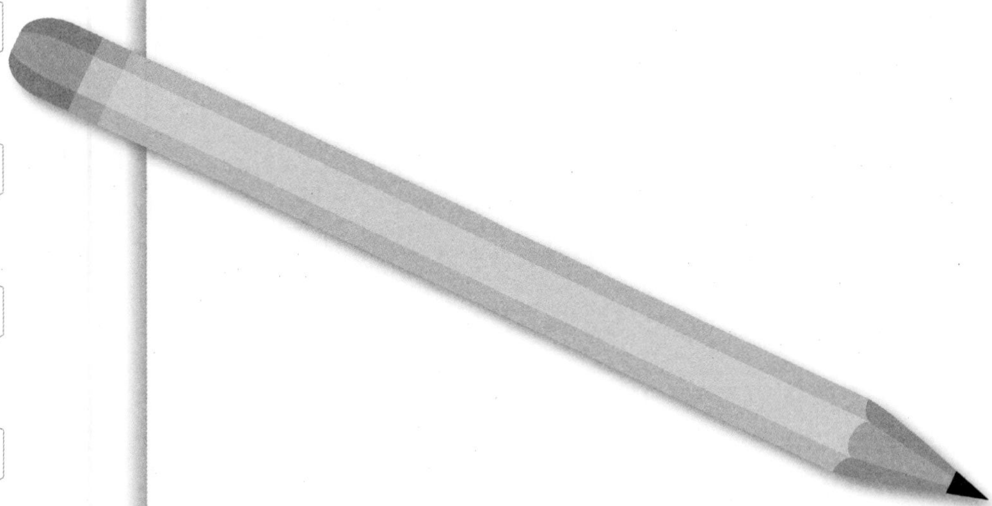

Name: ____________________ Date: __________

Directions: Color the chart to record the height of your first tower. Measure your new tower. Record its height. Then, circle the answer to each question.

10		
9		
8		
7		
6		
5		
4		
3		
2		
1		
Height (in inches)	**My First Tower**	**My New Tower**

1. Is your second tower taller than it is wide?
   yes **no**

2. Which tower is taller?

   My First Tower **My Second Tower**

Name: ______________________________ Date: ____________

Directions: Draw yourself as an engineer. Show how you built your tower.

Talk About It!

What did you achieve in this challenge?
What else do you want to build?

Pushes and Pulls Teaching Support

Overview of Unit Activities

Students will learn about and explore pushes and pulls through the following activities:

- studying pictures of pushes and pulls and answering questions
- drawing examples of pushes and pulls around them
- experimenting with using air to push and pull paper
- drawing designs for sails
- graphing pushes and pulls
- creating sails for wind-powered cars

Materials Per Group

Week 1

- paper
- straws

STEAM Challenge

- basic student materials
- construction paper (2+ pieces)
- craft sticks (10+)
- electric fan (1)
- felt and other fabric pieces (5)
- foil (10" x 10", 25 cm x 25 cm)
- prebuilt car bases (See Digital Resources for step-by-step instructions.)
- ruler or yardstick (1)
- tissue paper (2–3 sheets)

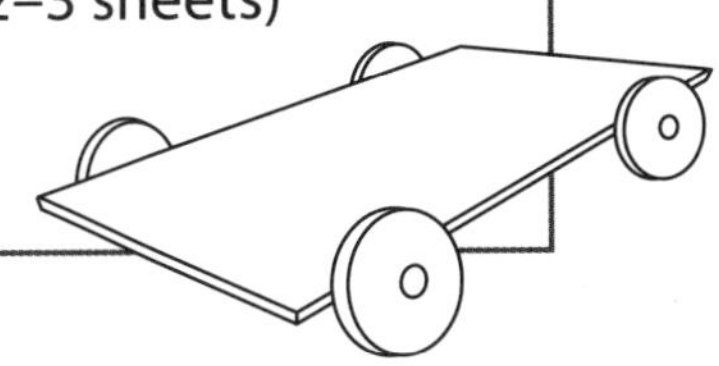

Setup and Instructional Tips

- **Week 1 Day 3:** Give each student a small piece of paper. Have them ball it up. Then, students can play with blowing and sucking air through straws to push and pull the paper balls.
- **Week 2 Day 1:** Read this challenge introduction to students. "Most cars need gas to run. It takes money to put gas in cars. Wind is free and will never run out. Your challenge is to make a toy car that uses wind to move. The base of the car is ready. You must make a sail to go on the car." Explain the challenge, the criteria, and the constraint.
- **Testing Days:** Set a fan just behind a starting line. Test multiple car designs at a time, depending on fan size. Turn on the fan, and see how far each car will go until it stops. Place a ruler or yardstick on the floor so students can observe and record distances traveled.
- **Testing Days:** If using metric measurements, you may wish to recreate the charts on pages 62 and 66 to include higher values.
- **Safety Note:** Keep students away from the fan blades and power source.

Discussion Questions

- How can we make objects move?
- Where do you see pushes and pulls at school and home?
- How can wind make things move?
- How well might a real, full-size wind-powered car work?
- How can testing and observing help you improve your designs?

Additional Notes

- **Possible Misconception:** A person must constantly push or pull an object to keep it moving.
  Truth: An initial push or pull can get an object moving. It may keep moving, even if a person is no longer touching an object.
- **Possible Design Solutions:** Students may choose to make one or multiple sails and mount them in a variety of places (sides, front, middle, and back) on the vehicle.

Scaffolding and Extension Suggestions

- To support measurement when testing sails, create a road of colored pieces of construction paper, each an inch (2.5 cm) in length. This will help students estimate how far each car travels.

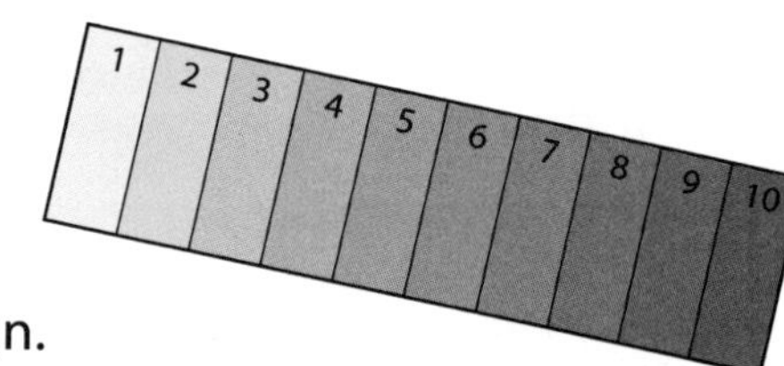

- Challenge students to change the car base during the redesign. Ask questions, such as "Do you want to change the number or placement of the wheels?" "What about the shape of the base?"

Answer Key

Week 1 Day 1

1. pull
2. push
3. push
4. pull

Week 1 Day 2

Charts should show everyday objects that can be pushed or pulled, such as chairs and doors.

Week 1 Day 3

1. Drawings should show paper balls moving away from the straws.
2. Drawings should show paper balls moving toward the straws.

Week 1 Day 4

Students should have drawings on their sails.

Week 1 Day 5

1. person throwing a ball

Weeks 2 & 3

See STEAM Challenge Rubric on page 221.

Name: ______________________ Date: ____________

Directions: Read the text. Look at the pictures. Then, circle *push* or *pull* for each image.

Objects can be moved with force. You can push them. You can pull them.

push

pull

1.

push **pull**

2.

push **pull**

3.

push **pull**

4.

push **pull**

Name: ______________________________ Date: _____________

Directions: Read the text. Look at the pictures. Then, find things around you that can be pushed. Find things that can be pulled. Draw them on the chart.

Pushes and pulls are all around you.

push

pull

Push	Pull

Name: ______________________________ Date: ____________

Directions: Blow air out of the straw. Then, suck air in. Blow soft. Blow hard. Move the paper ball around.

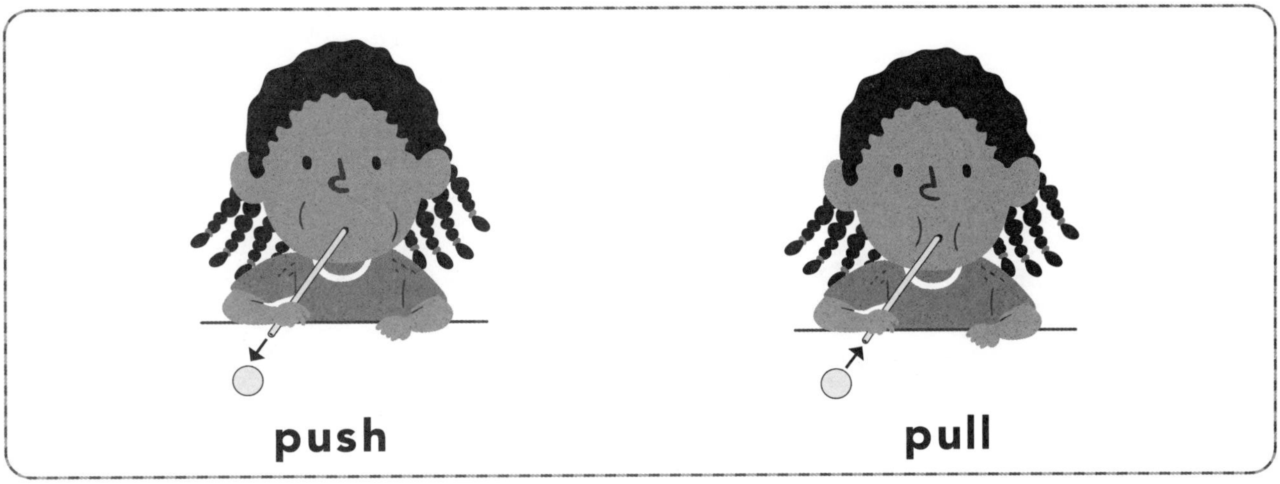

1. What happens when you blow air? Draw the ball. Draw an arrow to show which way it will go.

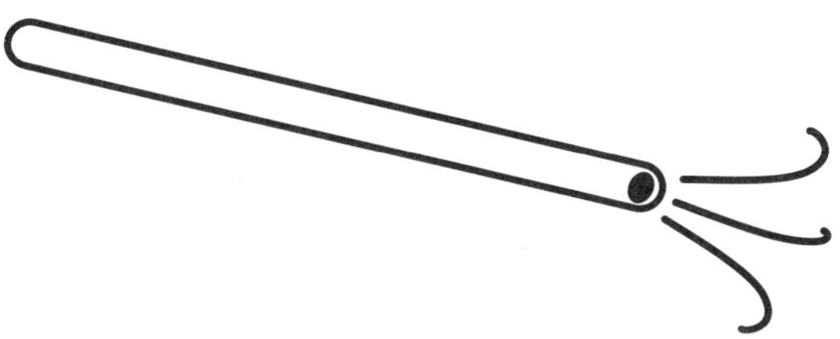

2. What happens when you suck air in? Draw the ball. Draw an arrow to show which way it will go.

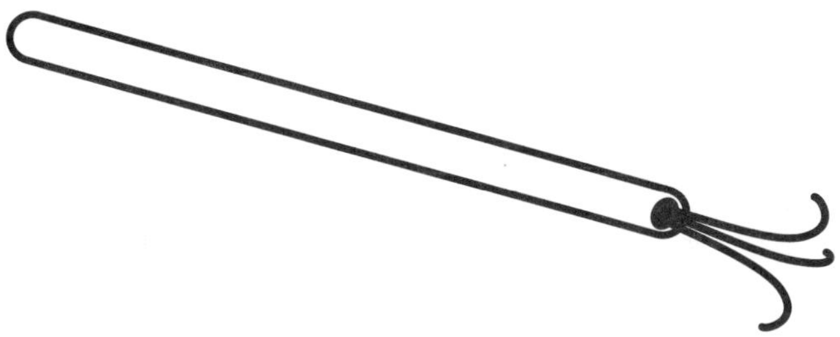

Name: ______________________________ Date: ____________

Directions: Sailboats use air to move. Wind can push them. Draw a design on these sails.

Wind blows against the sails. Wind pushes the boat in the water.

Name: ______________________________ Date: ____________

Directions: Count the pictures of pushes and pulls. Color the graph to show how many there are of each.

5				
4				
3				
2				
1				

1. Which push or pull had the most pictures?

Name: ______________________ Date: __________

Directions: Read the text. Then, label the parts of the wind-powered car.

The Challenge

Make a toy car that uses wind to move.

- **Criteria**—Your sail design must move the car forward using wind from a fan.
- **Constraint**—You may use only the materials given to you.

Word Bank

base mast sail wheel wind

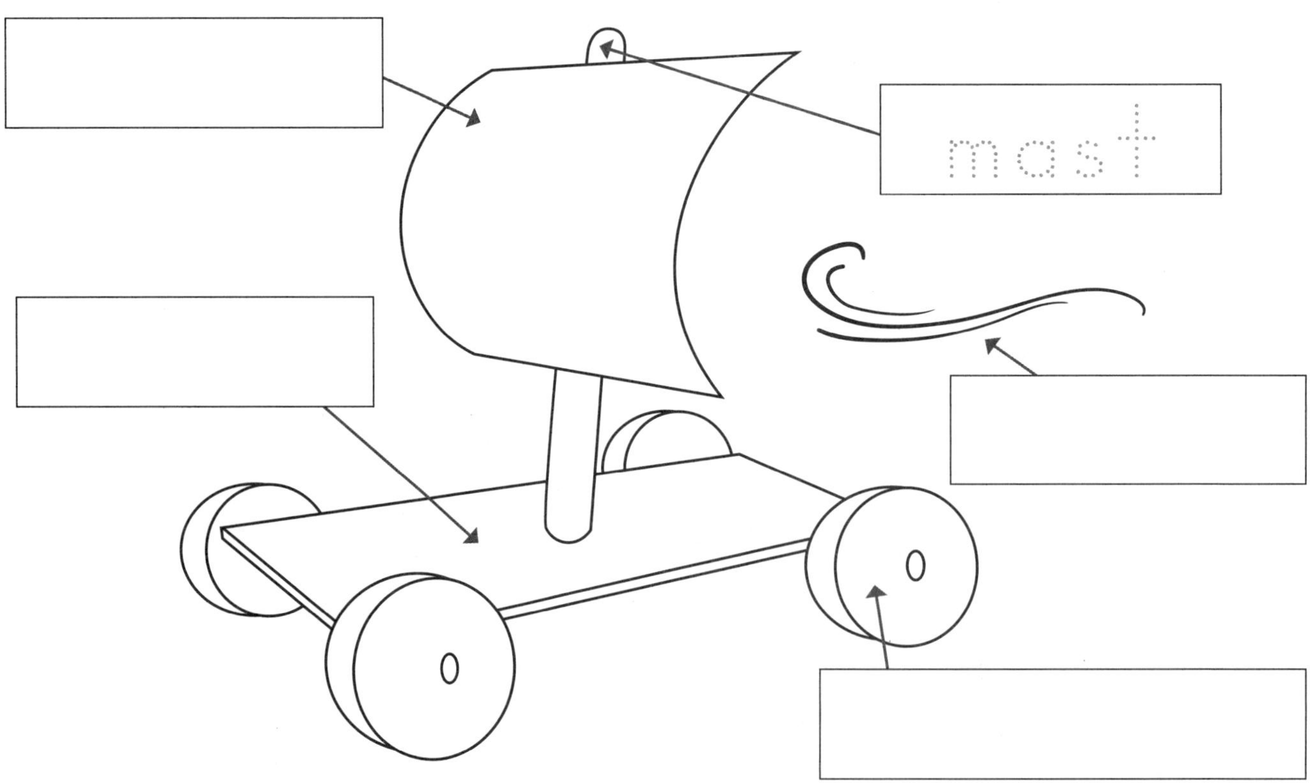

Name: ______________________________ Date: ____________

Directions: Read the questions. Circle the options you like.

1. How many sails will you have?

one two three four

2. What shape will the sails be?

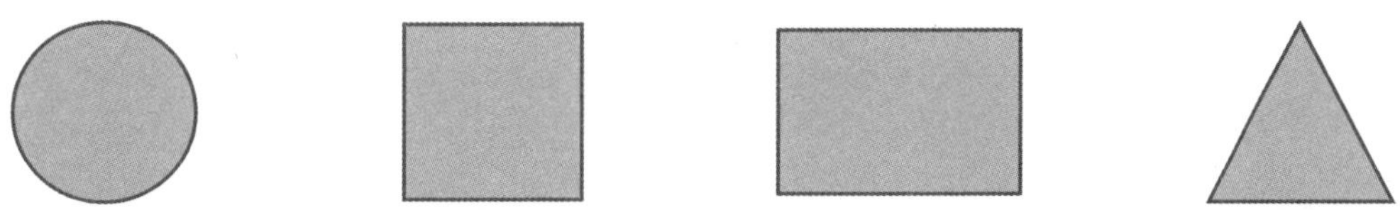

circle square rectangle triangle

3. How big will they be?

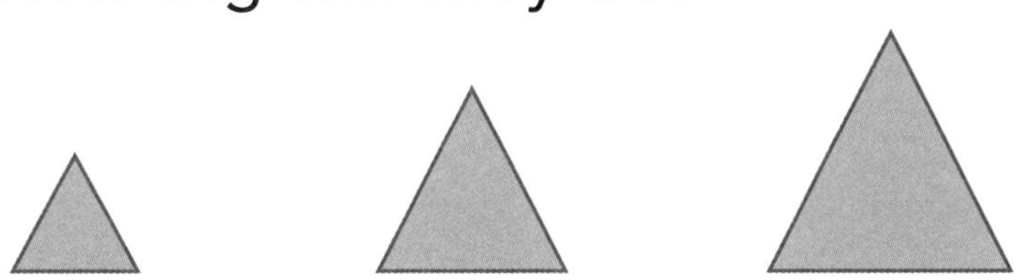

small medium large

4. What will you use for your sail?

paper fabric foil

Name: ______________________ Date: ____________

Directions: Sketch your sail or sails. Label the parts of your car.

Word Bank

base mast sail wheel wind

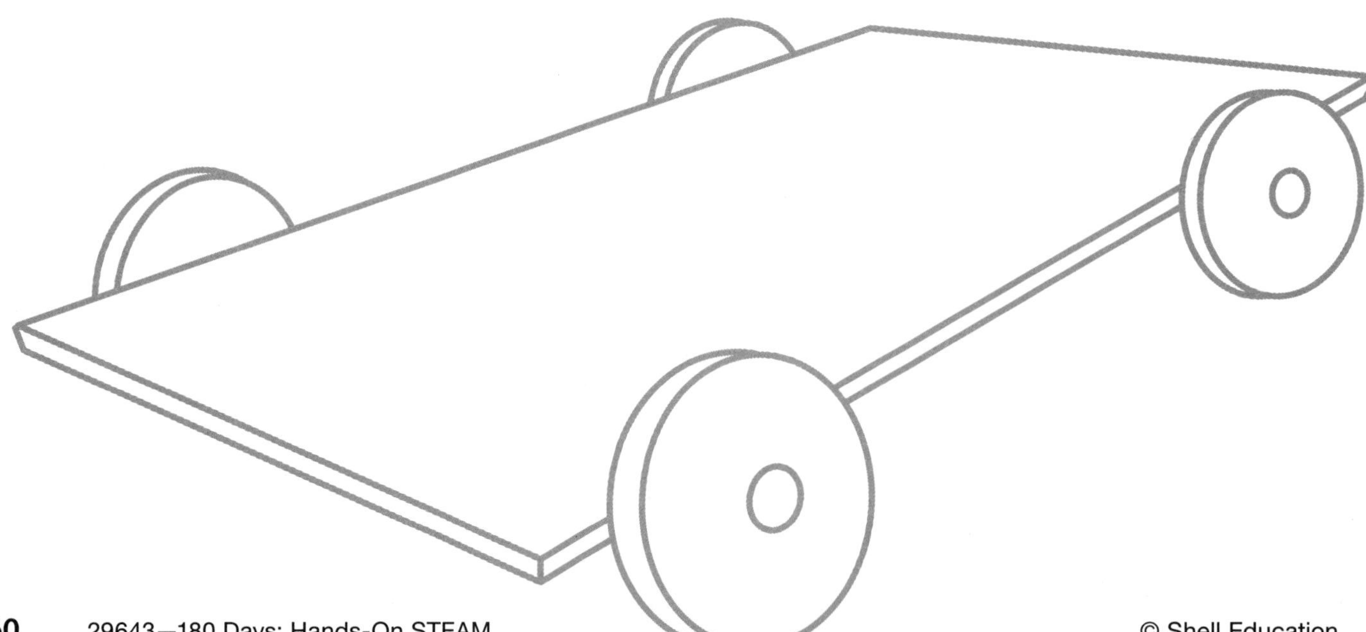

Name: ______________________________ Date: ____________

Directions: Build your wind-powered car. Check off the steps as you go.

- ☐ Look at your design sketch.
- ☐ Gather the materials you need.
- ☐ Attach your mast to the base.
- ☐ Cut out your sail.
- ☐ Attach the sail to the mast.
- ☐ Check that all parts are glued or taped well.

Quick Tip!

It is okay to change your design as you go!

Name: ______________________________ Date: ____________

Directions: Place your car on the ground. Turn on a fan. Keep it on until the car stops. Mark how far your car went. Test your car two times.

	How Many Inches Did It Move?									
	1	2	3	4	5	6	7	8	9	10+
Test 1										
Test 2										

Quick Tip!

Watch as others test their cars.
See how different sail designs work.

Name: ______________________________ Date: ____________

Directions: Think about your sail design. Answer the questions.

1. How well did your sail work?

2. Draw two sail designs that you saw from others. Put a checkmark by your favorite.

☐ **Design 1**	☐ **Design 2**

Name: ______________________________ Date: ____________

Directions: Plan your new design. Then, sketch your new design.

1. Will you change the number of sails?

   yes **no**

2. Will you change the shape of your sails?

   yes **no**

3. Will you change the size of your sails?

   yes **no**

4. Will you change the material of your sails?

   yes **no**

Try This!

Be creative! See how different you can make this design.

Name: ______________________________ Date: ____________

Directions: Rebuild the sails for your car. Make them work better. Use this list to help you.

- ☐ Look at your first design.
- ☐ Look at your plan to make it better.
- ☐ Get the materials you need.
- ☐ Take off parts you do not want.
- ☐ Add or make the changes you do want.
- ☐ Check that everything is glued or taped well.

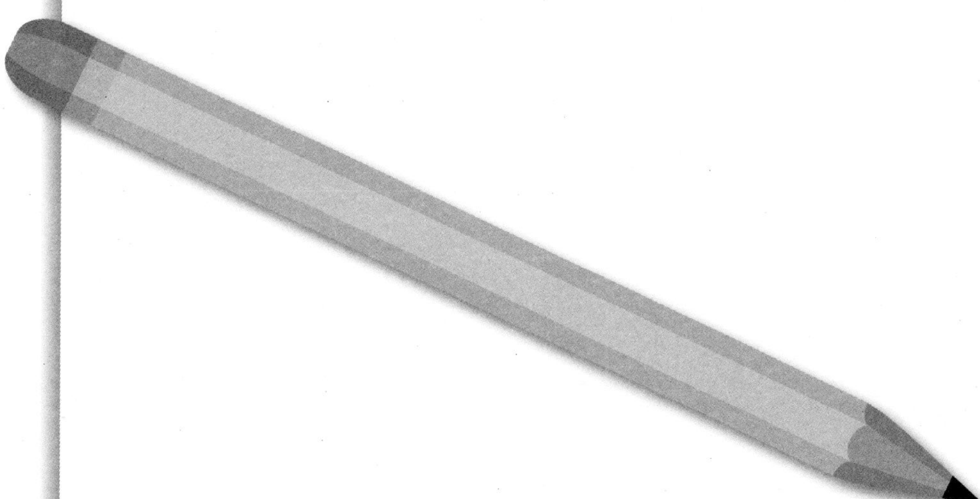

Name: ______________________ Date: __________

Directions: Place your car on the ground. Turn on a fan. Keep it on until the car stops. Mark how far your car went. Test your car two times.

	How Many Inches Did It Move?									
	1	2	3	4	5	6	7	8	9	10+
Test 1										
Test 2										

Did the car move farther this time?

yes **no**

Name: ______________________________ Date: ____________

Directions: Draw yourself as an engineer. Show how you worked on this challenge.

Talk About It!

What part of your design are you most proud of?
What surprised you about this challenge?

Animal Homes Teaching Support

Overview of Unit Activities

Students will learn about and explore animal homes through the following activities:

- reading about plant and animal needs
- matching animals to their homes
- searching for examples of animals and plants changing the environment
- designing new animals and showing their habitats
- creating animal homes

Materials Per Group

Week 1

- access to outdoor space or online search

STEAM Challenge

- basic student supplies
- clay
- fake feathers (5–10)
- natural materials (handful of each: dirt, leaves, twigs, branches, flowers, stones, seeds)
- string (2–5+ feet, 60–150+ cm)

Setup and Instructional Tips

- **Week 1 Day 4:** Students will be evaluating their designs. Discuss how real-world testing is not an option with this challenge because of the animals involved.
- **Week 2 Day 1:** Read this challenge introduction to students. "People live in homes. Our homes keep us warm and dry. Animals build homes, too. Their homes keep them safe and give their babies places to live. There are many types of animal homes. Your challenge will be to choose an animal and build a home, or model of a home, for it." Explain the challenge, the criteria, and the constraint.
- **Week 2 Day 3:** Discuss the materials that will be available for students before they begin their sketches.

Discussion Questions

- What do plants and animals need?
- Why do plants and animals change their environments?
- Why do different animals build different types of homes?
- What materials do animals use to build their homes?
- What type of home do you live in?
- How is your home like an animal's home? How is it different?

Additional Notes

- **Possible Misconception:** Animals change their environments, but plants do not.
  Truth: Plants can also change their environments. Point out examples on **Week 1 Day 3** as you explore outside.
- **Possible Misconception:** Homes of domesticated animals are examples of how animals change their environments.
  Truth: Homes for domesticated animals are often build by humans (dogs: doghouse, chickens: coop, pigs: pig sty, cows: barn).
- **Possible Design Solutions:** Students may model the animal homes after things they are already familiar with, such as human homes, birds' nests, or beaver dams.

Scaffolding and Extension Suggestions

- If examples of animals and plants changing their environments are hard to find on **Week 1 Day 3**, show students pictures online, such as a beaver dam and tree roots breaking through concrete.
- Challenge students to create homes that are waterproof or windproof in the redesign process.

Answer Key

Week 1 Day 1

1. water, space

Week 1 Day 2
Lines should be drawn connecting sea otter/kelp forest, eagle/nest, and sloth/tree.

Week 1 Day 3
Possible drawings: broken branch, hole in ground or tree, nest, roots of plant breaking through ground.

Week 1 Day 4
Student drawings should include original animals and their habitats.

Week 1 Day 5
The left side of the Venn should be colored yellow, the middle green, and the right side blue.

Weeks 2 & 3
See STEAM Challenge Rubric on page 221.

Name: ______________________ Date: __________

Directions: Read the text. Look at the chart. Then, circle the answers.

Plants and animals need things to live and grow. They live where they can get the things they need.

Plants Need	Animals Need
water light space 	food water shelter space 

1. What things do both plants and animals need?

water

food

light

space

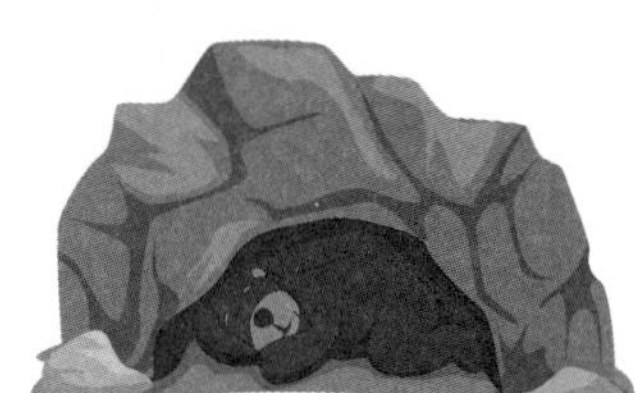

shelter

Name: ______________________ Date: __________

Directions: Read the text. Look at the pictures. Draw lines from animals to their plant homes.

Some animals make homes in plants. Some use parts of plants to make homes.

sea otter

eagle

sloth

tree

kelp forest

nest

Name: ______________________________ Date: ____________

Directions: Read the text. Then, walk outside. Look for ways plants and animals change the space around them. Draw at least one example.

Plants and animals change the environment. They can make it a better place for them to live.

Name: ______________________________ Date: ____________

Directions: Draw a new type of animal. Draw where it lives. Show all the things it needs.

Animal Needs			
food	water	space	shelter

Name: ______________________________ Date: ____________

Directions: Look at the Venn diagram. Color the plant needs side yellow. Color the animal needs side blue. Color the part with the needs of both green.

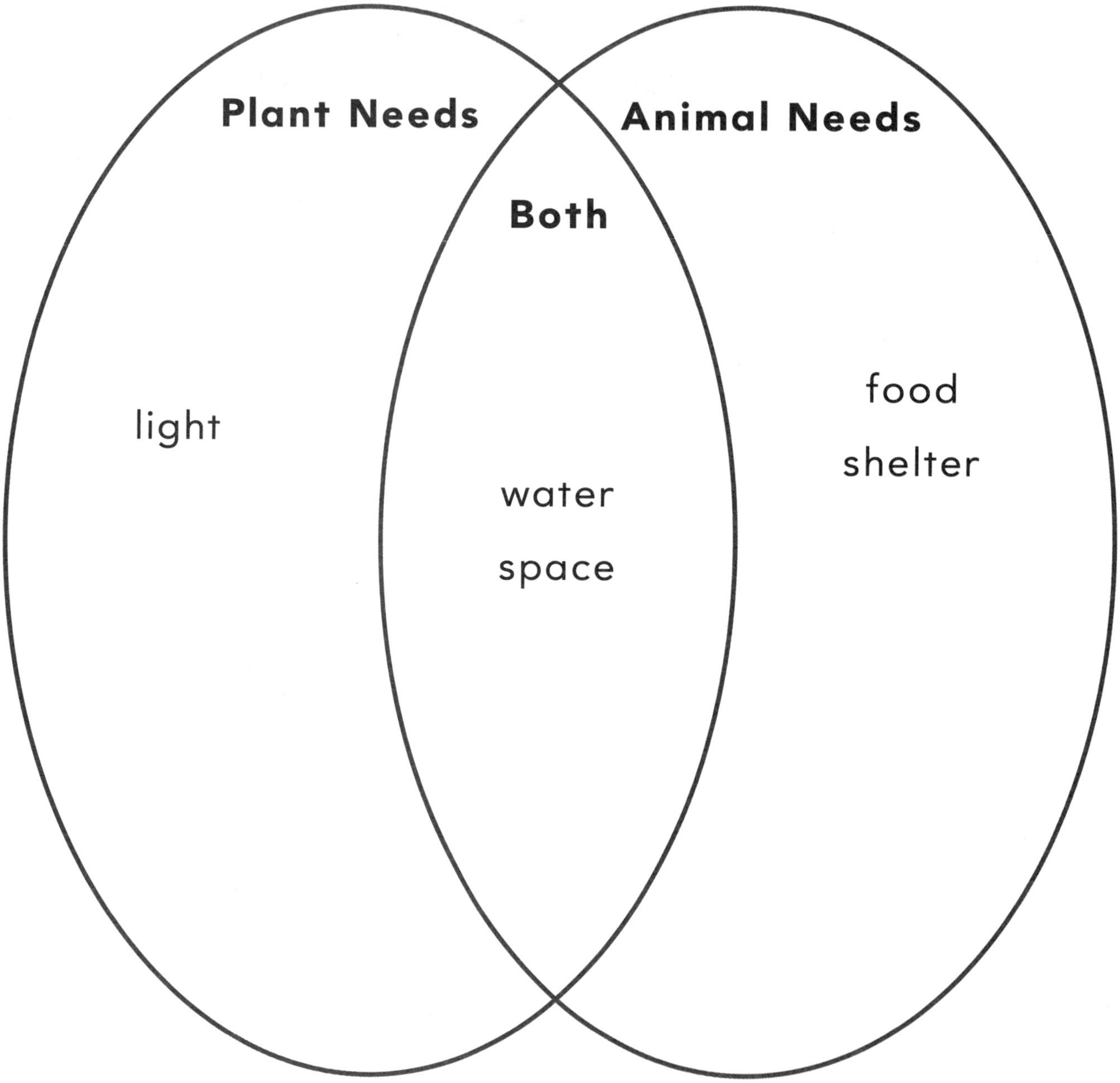

Talk About It!

What do you notice?

Name: ______________________ Date: __________

Directions: Read the text. Look at the pictures.

The Challenge

Build a home for an animal.

- **Criteria**—It must do all these things.
    - Keep the animal safe.
    - Keep the animal dry.
    - Keep the animal warm or cool.
    - Protect the babies.
- **Constraint**—Only use natural materials.

Talk About It!

What types of homes could you make for these animals?

Name: ______________________ Date: ____________

Directions: Read the text. Look at the animal homes. Mark the one you like the best.

Animal Home Ideas	
Prairie dogs dig tunnels. 	Hermit crabs find shells and carry them. 
Beavers build lodges with sticks. 	Wasps build hives. 
Puffins dig burrows. 	Swallows build nests with mud. 

Name: ______________________ Date: ____________

Directions: Circle an animal from the list. Think of where it lives. Sketch a home you will build for it.

beaver	lion
bird	snake
fox	spider
ladybug	your own idea

Think About It!

What materials will you need?

Name: ______________________ Date: ____________

Directions: Build your animal home. Check off the steps as you go. Complete the sentence.

- ☐ Look at your design sketch.
- ☐ Gather the materials you need.
- ☐ Build your animal home.
- ☐ Check that all parts are secured.

I built a home for a

____.

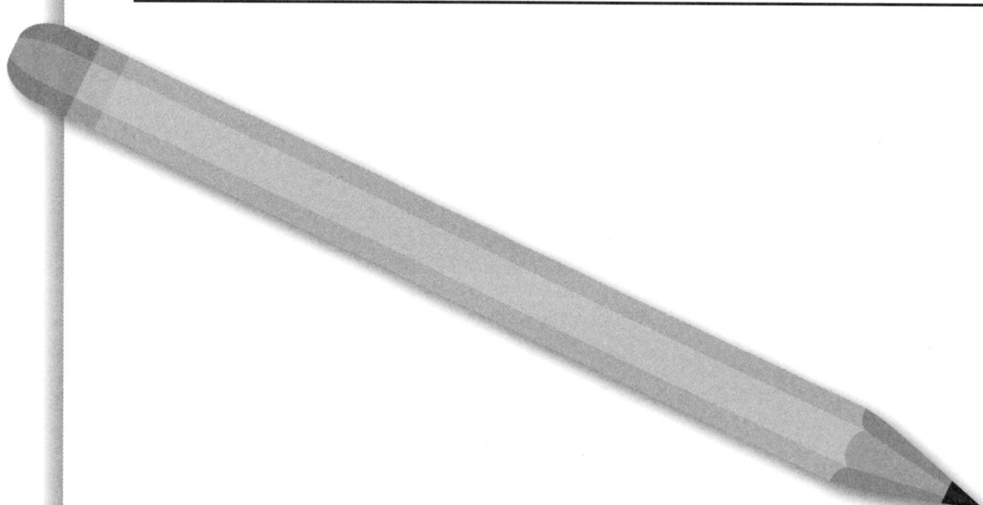

Name: ______________________________ Date: ____________

Directions: Check off what your home will do. Show it to others. Ask them the questions. Write or draw what they say.

- ☐ It will keep my animal safe.
- ☐ It will keep my animal dry.
- ☐ It will help keep my animal warm or cool.
- ☐ It will protect my animal's babies.

1. What part do you like best?

2. How can I make it better?

Name: ______________________ Date: __________

Directions: Think about your animal home design. Answer the questions.

1. How do you feel about the animal home you built?

2. Draw two animal homes you saw from others. Circle ideas you want to try in your animal home.

Design 1	Design 2

Think About It!

How can you make your animal home better?

Name: ______________________ Date: ____________

Directions: Plan your new design. Then, sketch your new design.

1. Will you make it bigger?

   yes **no**

2. Will you try new materials?

   yes **no**

3. Will you change the shape?

   yes **no**

Name: ______________________________ Date: ____________

Directions: Rebuild your animal home. Check off the steps as you go.

- ☐ Look at your design sketch.
- ☐ Gather the materials you need.
- ☐ Build your home.
- ☐ Check that all parts are secured.

Quick Tip!

You do not have to start from scratch! Make changes to your first animal home.

Name: ______________________ Date: __________

Directions: Check off what your home will do. Show it to others. Tell them how you made it better.

- ☐ It will keep my animal safe.
- ☐ It will keep my animal dry.
- ☐ It will help keep my animal warm or cool.
- ☐ It will protect my animal's babies.

Name: ______________________ Date: ____________

Directions: Draw a hard part of this challenge. Draw a fun part.

Hard

Fun

Talk About It!

What do you think an animal would say about the home you made?

Living and Nonliving Things Teaching Support

Overview of Unit Activities

Students will learn about and explore living and nonliving things through the following activities:

- reading about living and nonliving things
- drawing examples of living and nonliving things
- experimenting with living and nonliving things
- designing their own plants and showing how they grow
- analyzing a chart showing plant growth
- creating new products inspired by living things

Materials Per Group

Week 1

- active dry yeast (1 spoonful)
- apple juice (4 tbsp, 60 mL)
- jars (2+)
- sand (1 spoonful)

STEAM Challenge

- basic school supplies
- common recycled goods (2–4 empty food containers, cardboard tubes, recycled paper, plastic bottles, bottle caps, etc.)
- other materials for students to choose from (see Additional Notes section)

Setup and Instructional Tips

- **Week 1 Day 3:** Each jar should contain 1 spoonful of yeast or 1 spoonful of sand. After students draw the jars, add 2 tablespoons (30 mL) of apple juice to each jar and wait for results. You will need to wait about 15 minutes after combining ingredients to see growth and bubbles in the yeast jar(s).
- **Week 2 Day 1:** Read this challenge introduction to students. "Humans use ideas they see from other living things. Copying designs found in nature has given us a lot of great technologies. They help people solve problems or fill needs. Your challenge is to create something new that is inspired by a plant or animal." Explain the challenge, the criteria, and the constraint.

Discussion Questions

- How can you tell if something is living or nonliving?
- What does it mean to be a living thing?
- How do humans use ideas from nature to create new things?
- What things do you know of that might be inspired from nature?
- How can sharing and evaluating help you improve your design?

Additional Notes

- **Materials:** This challenge is very open-ended. Students choose what products they will make. You may want to ask students which materials they might want and provide them at your discretion.
- **Possible Misconception:** Living things need to currently be alive.
  Truth: Something is classified as living if it is or has ever been alive.
- **Possible Student Design Solutions:** Students may take inspiration from how animals move, what their skin looks and feels like, how they keep warm or cool, and how plant and animal shapes help them.

Scaffolding and Extension Suggestions

- Support students with ideas for the challenge by doing a whole-class brainstorming session and looking for ideas online.
- Challenge students by adding design criteria during Week 3, such as making their designs waterproof or making sure they do not blow over in strong wind.

Answer Key

Week 1 Day 1

1. circle cat; *X* on pencil
2. *X* on socks; circle tree
3. *X* on phone; circle snake
4. circle bee; *X* on toothbrush

Week 1 Day 2

Drawing examples: Living—plants, people, animals; Nonliving—pencil, desk, carpet, clock

Week 1 Day 3

Drawings should show the jars of sand and yeast before and after adding apple juice. The After drawing of yeast should show growth and bubbles. The sand jar should show just sand and apple juice.

Week 1 Day 5

1. B
2. A

Weeks 2 & 3

See STEAM Challenge Rubric on page 221.

Name: ______________________ Date: ____________

Directions: Read the text. For each row, circle the thing that is living. Write an *X* on the thing that is nonliving.

Living things are alive. They can grow and move. People are living things. Animals are living things. Plants are living things. Nonliving things do not grow. They do not move on their own.

1\.

cat

pencil

2\.

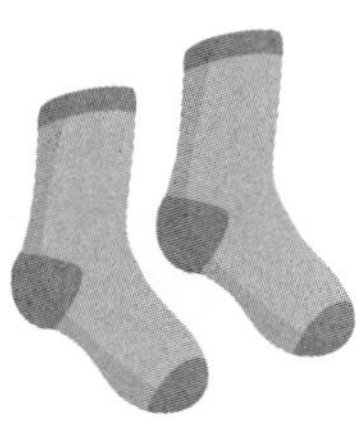

socks

tree

3\.

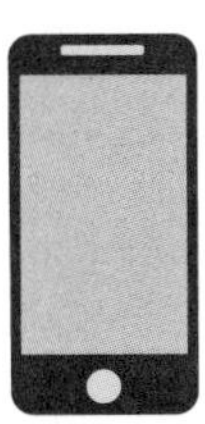

phone

snake

4\.

bee

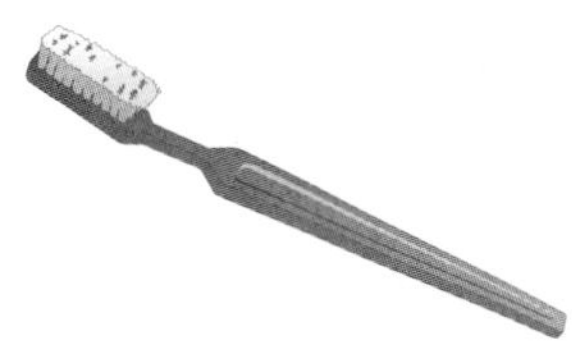

toothbrush

Name: ______________________ Date: __________

Directions: Read the text. Then, look around you. Find examples of living things. Find examples of nonliving things. Draw them on the chart.

What Do Living Things Do?

- They eat or make food.
- They grow.
- They move.
- They reproduce.

Living Things	Nonliving Things

Name: ______________________________ Date: ____________

Directions: Draw the sand and yeast in the top two jars. Add apple juice to each jar. The apple juice is food. Wait 15 minutes. Then, draw the jars again.

	Sand	**Yeast**
Before		
After		

Talk About It!

Which one is alive?
How can you tell?

Name: ______________________________ Date: ____________

Directions: Imagine you go for a hike. You find a new plant. No one has seen it before. Draw what it looks like when it is young. Draw what it looks like after it grows.

Name: ______________________ Date: __________

Directions: Read the text. Look at the chart. Answer the questions.

Raul plants a seed in his garden. He checks it every month. He records how many leaves the plant has.

1. When did the plant have the most leaves?

(A) April

(B) July

2. In May, there were ________ leaves.

(A) 2

(B) 5

Name: ______________________ Date: ____________

Directions: Read the text. Then, match each object to the living thing it was inspired by.

The Challenge

Make a new product. Get an idea from a living thing. It can be a tool. It can be a toy. It can be a piece of clothing.

- **Criteria**—It must be inspired by nature. It must have a purpose.
- **Constraint**—You may only use the materials given to you.

animal toy

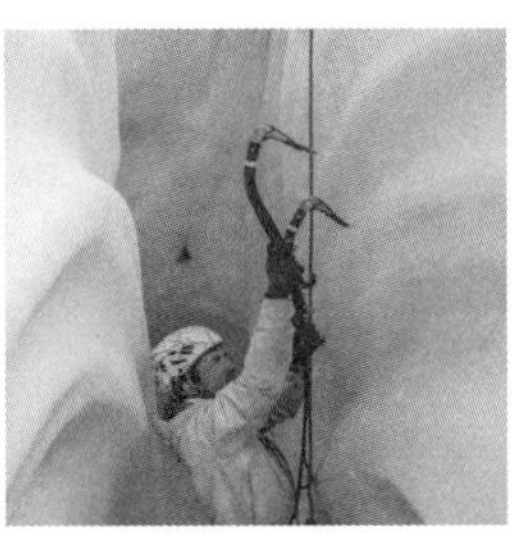
climbing tool

bookshelf

Name: ______________________ Date: ____________

Directions: Look at the living things. Draw ideas you get from them for new products. Share your ideas with others.

Living Thing	My Ideas

Talk About It!

What do you want to make?
What will it do?

Name: ______________________ Date: __________

Directions: Think about your product. Answer the question. Draw the living thing that gave you the idea. Sketch your product.

1. What will you make?

a tool a toy a piece of clothing

My Product

Living Thing

Name: ______________________ Date: __________

Directions: Build your product. Check off the steps as you go.

- [ ] Look at your design sketch.
- [ ] Think about what inspired your design.
- [ ] Gather the materials you need.
- [ ] Build your design.
- [ ] Decorate your design.
- [ ] Check that all parts are glued or taped well.

Quick Tip!

It is okay to change your design as you go!

Name: ______________________________ Date: ____________

Directions: Show your product to others. Tell them about it. Ask them questions. Write or draw what they say.

Tell

1. Tell what idea you used from nature.
2. Tell how people can use it.
3. Tell who would want to use it.

Ask

4. What do you like?

5. How can I make it better?

Name: ______________________________ Date: ____________

Directions: Think about the product you made. Answer the questions.

1. How do you feel about what you made?

2. Did it turn out how you planned?

yes **no**

3. Draw what you like best about it.

Name: ______________________________ Date: ____________

Directions: Plan your new design. Then, sketch your new design.

Think About It!

How can you make it work better?
How can you make it look nicer?

Name: ______________________________ Date: ____________

Directions: Rebuild your product inspired by nature. Check off the steps as you go.

- ☐ Look at your design sketch.
- ☐ Think about what inspired your design.
- ☐ Gather the materials you need.
- ☐ Build your design.
- ☐ Decorate your design.
- ☐ Check that all parts are glued or taped well.

Quick Tip!

If something is not working, try different materials!

Name: ______________________________ Date: ______________

Directions: Show your product to others. Tell them about it. Ask them questions. Write or draw what they say.

Tell

1. Explain what your product is.
2. Tell what living thing gave you this idea.
3. Tell how people can use it.
4. Tell who would want to use it.

Ask

5. What do you like about my new design?

6. Would you use my product?

Name: ______________________ Date: __________

Directions: Draw someone using your new product.

Talk About It!

What did you do well in this challenge?
What ideas do you have for other products?

The Five Senses Teaching Support

Overview of Unit Activities

Students will learn about and explore the five senses through the following activities:

- reading about and studying pictures of the five senses
- drawing pictures of how we use sound to learn about and observe the world
- experimenting with making sound vibrations
- listening to music and drawing reactions
- analyzing data about sound made in glass bottles
- creating sound mufflers

Materials Per Group

Week 1

- four songs of different genres (e.g., classical, pop, country, reggae)
- rubber band (1)

STEAM Challenge

- basic school supplies
- bubble wrap (10" x 10", 25 cm x 25 cm)
- cardboard tubes (1–3)
- coffee filters (3–5)
- cotton balls (10+)
- egg carton (1)
- foam paper (1 sheet)
- packing peanuts (1–2 handfuls)

Setup and Instructional Tips

- **Week 1 Day 3:** Give each student group a rubber band. Have one student stretch the rubber band between their thumbs. Have the other students gently pluck the rubber band.
- **Week 1 Day 4:** Take turns playing each song. Allow time for students to draw things inspired by each type of music.
- **Week 2 Day 1:** Read this challenge introduction to students. "Has anyone ever told you to be quiet? Or maybe you have wanted to block a sound. Your challenge is to create a sound muffler. It should absorb or block sound when you are talking." Explain the challenge, the criteria, and the constraint.

Discussion Questions

- What are the five senses?
- How do your five senses help you learn about the world around you?
- How does sound travel?
- How do the sound mufflers help block the sound?
- Where do you see things that muffle sound in the world around you?

Additional Notes

- **Possible Misconception:** Sound can only travel through the air.
  Truth: Sound can travel through all states of matter (solid, liquid, gas).
- **Possible Design Solutions:** Students may build tubes and stuff them with materials to block the sound.

Scaffolding and Extension Suggestions

- Support students with understanding how the amount of water inside each bottle changes the pitch on **Week 1 Day 5** by demonstrating using real bottles and water.
- Challenge students with an additional engineering challenge—to make sound amplifiers or things that will make the sound louder.

Answer Key

Week 1 Day 1

1. B
2. A

Week 1 Day 2

Student answers should show what everyone observes with their senses. Examples: see—bird or people at picnic; smell—grill or food; taste—hamburger; hear—music from bird; touch—dog

Week 1 Day 3

Drawings may include speakers, headphones, animals, cars, etc.

Week 1 Day 5

1. A
2. B

Weeks 2 & 3

See STEAM Challenge Rubric on page 221.

Name: ______________________ Date: ____________

Directions: Read the text. Answer the questions.

Humans have five senses. We use them to learn about the world. We use different parts of our bodies for each sense.

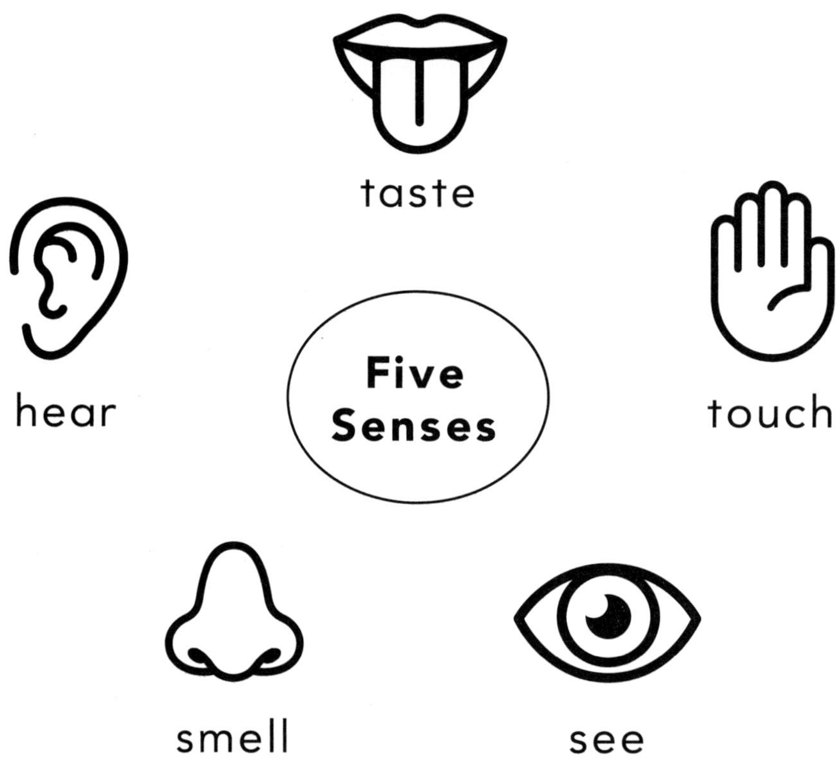

1. How many senses do humans have?

Ⓐ 6

Ⓑ 5

2. Which body part do you use to smell?

Ⓐ nose

Ⓑ eye

Name: ______________________ Date: ____________

Directions: Read the text. Draw an arrow from each question to an answer.

Our senses help us. We use our senses to learn. They keep us safe. They help us have fun. Sometimes we use one. Sometimes, we use them all at once.

What do they smell?

What do they hear?

What does the boy taste?

What does the girl see?

What does the older girl touch?

Name: ______________________ Date: ____________

Directions: Read about sound. Do the activities.

We can hear sound. Sound is made of waves. Sound waves are made when things move back and forth quickly. This is called *vibration.*

- Put your hand on your throat. Hum. Can you feel it?
- Use a rubber band to create sound vibrations.

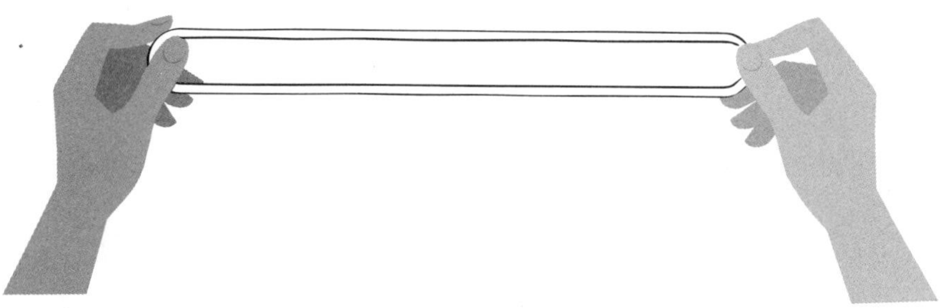

1. Draw other things that make sound.

Name: ______________________ Date: ____________

Directions: Listen to the music. Draw what each song makes you think of or feel.

Song 1	Song 2
Song 3	**Song 4**

Name: ______________________ Date: __________

Directions: Read the text. Look at the pictures. Answer the questions.

If you tap a glass, the air inside will vibrate. Air in an empty glass vibrates slowly. This makes a low sound. Air in a full glass vibrates fast. This makes a high sound.

1. Which glass will have the highest sound?

(A) glass A

(B) glass B

2. Which glass will have the lowest sound?

(A) glass A

(B) glass C

Name: ______________________ Date: __________

Directions: Read the text. Then, look at sound mufflers in real life. Circle the ones you have seen or used.

The Challenge

Make a voice muffler to block sound. Work with a partner.

- **Criteria**—Your partner should not be able to understand the sentence you say.
- **Constraint**—You may only use the materials given to you.

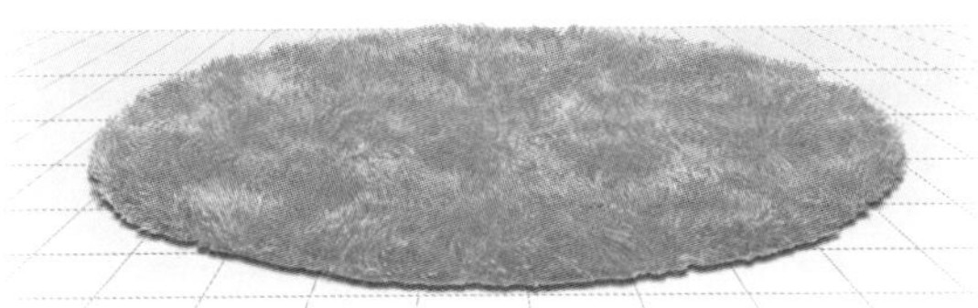

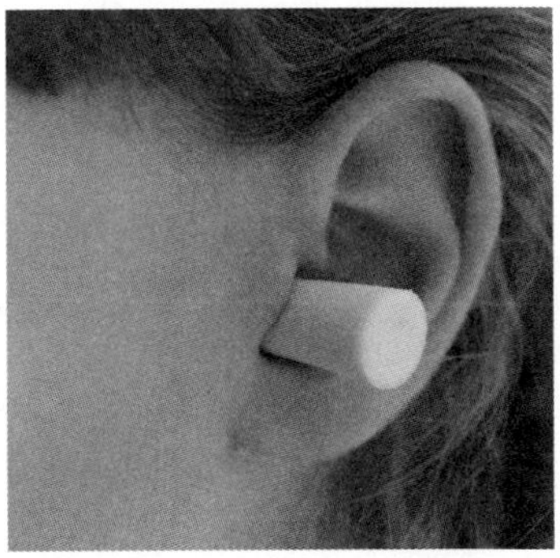

Name: ______________________________ Date: ____________

Directions: Read the questions. Talk to others about ideas. Circle the options you like.

1. What shape will it be?

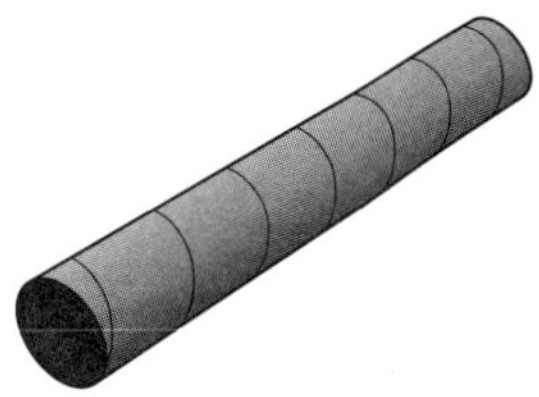

2. You need materials to absorb and block sound. Which ones will you put in your voice muffler?

Talk About It!

Where will you talk into the voice muffler? Where will someone listen?

Name: ______________________ Date: __________

Directions: Sketch your voice muffler. Label the parts.

Word Bank

frame   material   sound in   sound out

Name: ______________________________ Date: ____________

Directions: Build your voice muffler. Check off the steps as you go.

- ☐ Look at your design sketch.
- ☐ Gather the materials you need.
- ☐ Build a frame for your sound muffler.
- ☐ Add sound-absorbing material.
- ☐ Check that it doesn't fall out.
- ☐ Check that all parts are glued or taped well.

Quick Tip!

It is okay to do a few mini tests as you build!

Name: ______________________________ Date: ____________

Directions: Test your muffler. Take turns. One partner talks into the voice muffler. They should say a sentence. The other partner should listen. Rate how well it worked.

1. How well could your partner understand you?

0	1	2	3	4	5
not at all					really well

2. How well could you hear your partner?

0	1	2	3	4	5
not at all					really well

Name: ______________________ Date: ____________

Directions: Think about your voice muffler design. Answer the questions.

1. How well did your voice muffler work?

2. Draw two voice muffler designs that you saw from others. Put a checkmark by your favorite.

☐ **Design 1**	☐ **Design 2**

Name: ______________________ Date: ____________

Directions: Sketch your new design. Circle the parts or materials that are different.

Name: ______________________ Date: ____________

Directions: Rebuild your voice muffler. Check off the steps as you go.

- ☐ Look at your design sketch.
- ☐ Gather the materials you need.
- ☐ Think about what you learned when you built your first design.
- ☐ Rebuild your design. Make the changes you want.
- ☐ Check that all parts are glued or taped well.

Name: ______________________ Date: ____________

Directions: Retest your muffler. Take turns. One partner talks into the voice muffler. They should say a sentence. The other partner should listen. Rate how well it worked.

1. How well could your partner understand you?

0	1	2	3	4	5
not at all					really well

2. How well could you hear your partner?

0	1	2	3	4	5
not at all					really well

Talk About It!

Did the new design work better?

Name: ______________________________ Date: ______________

Directions: Draw something you learned from the challenge. Write what you learned.

Talk About It!

What part of your design are you most proud of?
What surprised you about this challenge?

Plants Teaching Support

Overview of Unit Activities

Students will learn about and explore what plants need to live and grow through the following activities:

- reading about and studying a diagram of how plants get what they need
- reading about and studying pictures of unique plant parts
- examining the seeds of different fruits
- designing vegetable gardens
- analyzing a graph showing the number of seeds found in fruit
- building seed dispersal devices

Materials Per Group

Week 1

- pieces of fruit with seeds (4 different types)

STEAM Challenge

- balloons (2)
- basic school supplies
- cardboard tubes (2)
- clothespins (3–4)
- coffee filters (2)
- cotton balls (10)
- plastic wrappers (2–3)
- recycled cardboard boxes of various sizes (juice, cereal, crackers, etc.; 2)
- recycled plastic containers (2)
- seeds, such as sunflower or beans (1–2)
- string (4 feet, 1.2 m)

Setup and Instructional Tips

- **Before the Unit:** Send notes home asking students to bring in natural and commonly found materials, such as twigs, leaves, and grass to build their seed dispersal systems.
- **Week 1 Day 3:** Have an adult cut the fruit for students.
- **Week 2 Day 1:** Read this challenge introduction to students. "Seeds need to move to new places to grow. They cannot all grow in the same spot. Sometimes, humans help by planting seeds. But it must happen naturally, too. Your challenge will be to help a seed move from one place to another." Explain the challenge, the criteria, and the constraint.
- **Week 2 Day 3:** Discuss the materials that will be available for students before they begin their sketches.

Discussion Questions

- What do plants need to live, grow, and reproduce?
- How do plants adapt to meet their needs?
- How are seeds dispersed?
- Why are seeds important?
- How does comparing and testing your design help you improve it?

Additional Notes

- **Possible Misconception:** Plants don't respond to their environments.
  Truth: Plants do respond (e.g., leaves turn toward the sun, flowers bloom on days with more light, roots grow toward moisture).
- **Possible Design Solutions:** Students might attach balloons to help seeds float, make parachutes or paper airplanes to move seeds with the wind, or build structures covered in cotton balls to make seeds stick to them.

Scaffolding and Extension Suggestions

- Support students in generating ideas for their seed dispersal systems by showing them pictures and videos of examples online.
- Challenge students to design and build seed dispersal systems that use two ways to disperse the seeds.

Answer Key

Week 1 Day 1

1. A
2. B

Week 1 Day 2

Students should mark their favorite plant.

Week 1 Day 3

Student sketches should show fruits and their seeds.

Week 1 Day 5

1. 5
2. peach
3. pumpkin

Weeks 2 & 3

See STEAM Challenge Rubric on page 221.

Name: ______________________________ Date: ____________

Directions: Read the text. Look at the picture. Answer the questions.

Plants need air. Plants need water. Plants need light. Plants need space to grow. Plants need nutrients. Plants have parts that help them get what they need.

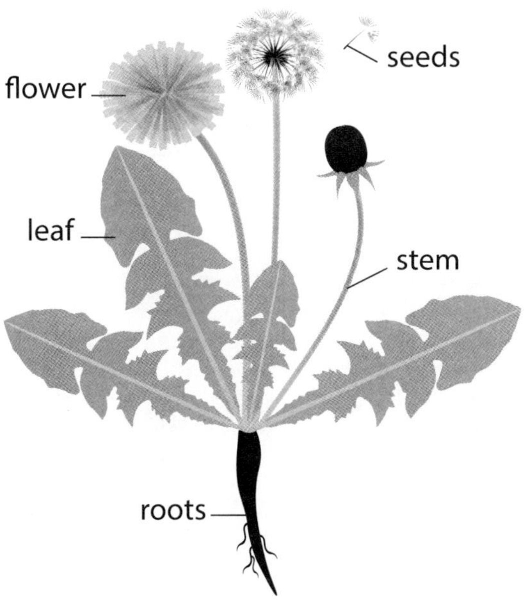

flowers—attract birds

seeds—can grow into new plants

leaf—makes food for the plant

stem—carries water from the roots and supports the plant

roots—get water and nutrients from soil

1. What can grow into a new plant?

Ⓐ a seed

Ⓑ a leaf

2. What parts get water from soil?

Ⓐ flowers

Ⓑ roots

Name: ______________________________ Date: ____________

Directions: Read the text. Look at the pictures. Mark your favorite plant.

Some plants must work hard to get what they need. They have special parts. They do special things.

Pitcher Plants	**Corpse Flower**
They hold water. Insects fall in. They give the plants nutrients. 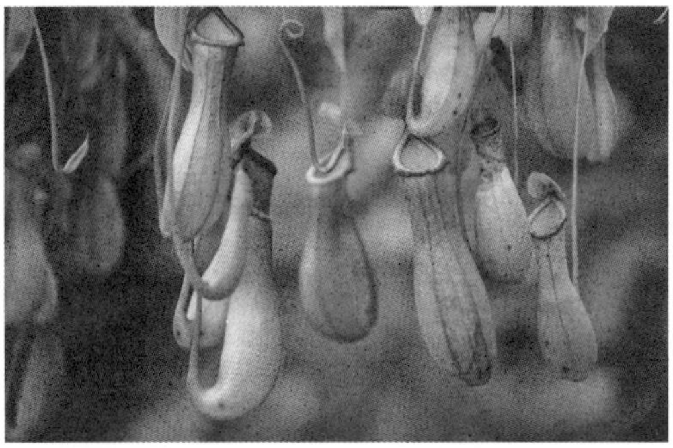	It stinks! This smell brings flies and beetles. They help it grow seeds. 
Giant Water Lily	**Living Stones**
The leaves are on top of the water. They are huge. 	They look like small rocks. Animals do not eat them. 

Name: ______________________ Date: __________

Directions: Plants make seeds to grow new plants. Seeds can be in fruit. Get four different types of fruit. Draw each fruit. Ask an adult to cut it for you. Then, draw the seeds.

Fruit	Seeds

Fruit	Seeds

Fruit	Seeds

Fruit	Seeds

Talk About It!

What do you notice?

Name: ______________________________ Date: ____________

Directions: Design a garden to grow fruits and vegetables.

Think About It!

What vegetables will you grow? What fruits will you grow? Where will you put the hose? Where will you sit?

Name: ______________________________ Date: ______________

Directions: Study the graph. It shows how many seeds were found in each fruit. Answer the questions.

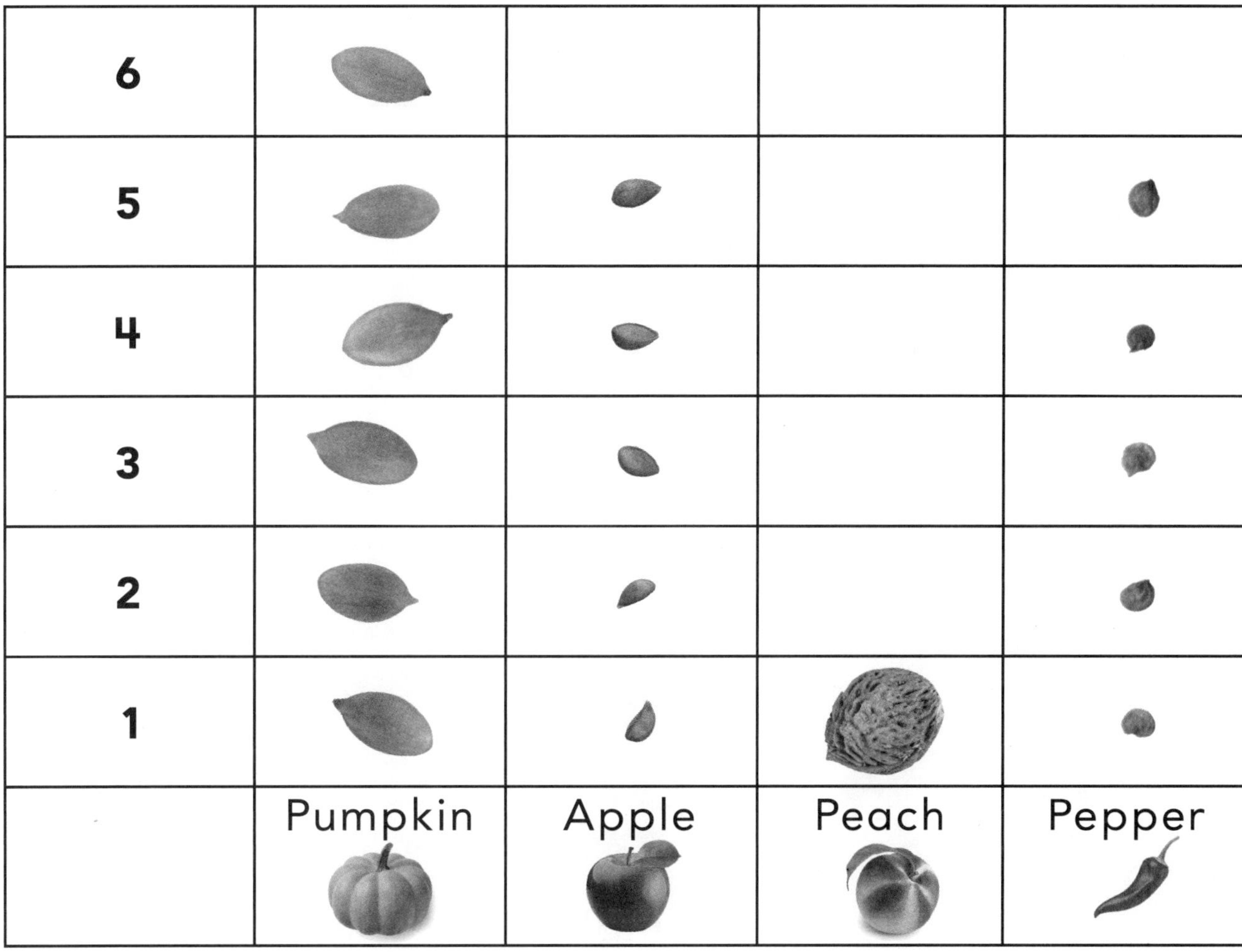

1. How many seeds were in the pepper? ______________

2. Which fruit had only 1 seed?

____

3. Which fruit had the most seeds?

____

Name: ______________________ Date: __________

Directions: Read the text. Then, circle or write the type of seed you will try to move.

The Challenge

Build a seed-moving device.

- **Criteria**—The device must move a seed from one place to another.
- **Constraint**—You may use only the materials you are given.

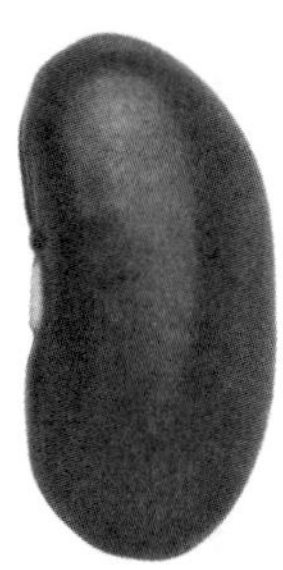

bean

pumpkin

sunflower

____

other: ______________________________

Think About It!

What are some materials you might use to build your device?

How could you attach or carry your seed?

Name: ______________________________ Date: ____________

Directions: Read the text. Look at the pictures. Then, mark which type of seed mover you will build.

Explosion

Pea and bean plants have pods. The seeds burst out when they are ready.

Water

Some seeds float. Water carries them to new places.

Wind

Some seeds catch rides on the wind.

Attachment

Some seeds get caught on animal fur and feathers.

Name: ______________________________ Date: _____________

Directions: Sketch your seed mover. Show how it will move a seed from place to place.

Quick Tip!

Are you stuck? Ask an adult to help you find ideas online. See what others have done.

Name: ______________________ Date: ____________

Directions: Build your seed mover. Check off the steps as you go.

- [ ] Look at the seed.
- [ ] Look at your design sketch.
- [ ] Gather the materials you need.
- [ ] Cut and attach the parts you need.
- [ ] Check that all parts are glued or taped well.
- [ ] Check that the seed will stay attached.

Quick Tip!

It is okay to change your design as you go!

Name: ______________________________ Date: ____________

Directions: Show your seed mover to others. Tell them about it. Show how it works. Ask them some questions. Write or draw what they say.

Tell

1. Tell how it moves a seed.
2. Explain why you designed it this way.

Show

3. Model how it works.
4. Did it move the seed from one place to another?

   yes **no**

Ask

5. What do you like?

6. How can I make it better?

Name: ______________________ Date: ____________

Directions: Think about your seed mover design. Answer the questions.

1. How well did your seed mover work?

2. Draw two designs that you saw from others. Put a checkmark by the one that worked best.

☐ **Design 1**	☐ **Design 2**

Name: ______________________________ Date: ____________

Directions: Plan your new design. Then, sketch your new design.

Try This!

Be creative! See how different you can make this design.

1. Will you change or add materials?

   yes **no**

2. Will you change the shape of your seed mover?

   yes **no**

Name: ______________________ Date: ____________

Directions: Rebuild your seed mover. Check off the steps as you go.

- ☐ Look at the seed.
- ☐ Look at your new design sketch.
- ☐ Gather the materials you need.
- ☐ Rebuild your seed mover. Make the changes you want.
- ☐ Check that all parts are attached.
- ☐ Check that the seed will stay attached.

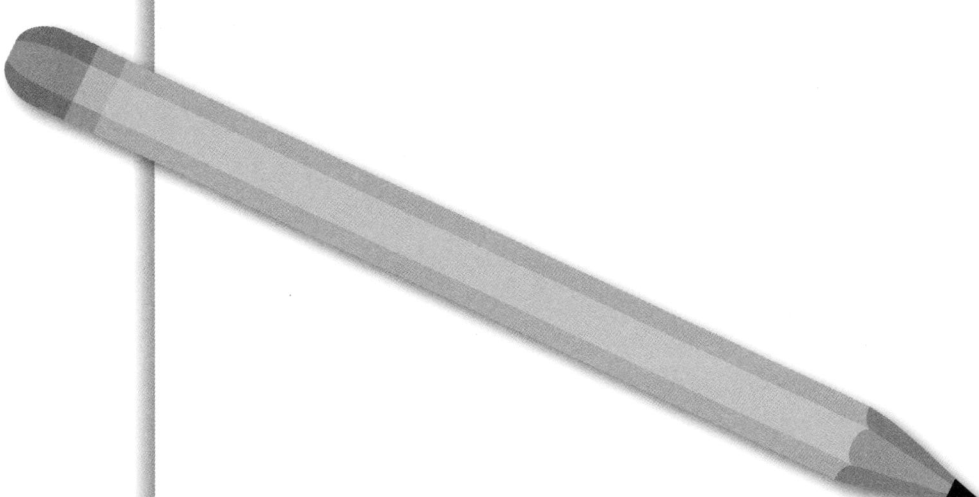

Name: ______________________ Date: __________

Directions: Show your seed mover to others. Tell them about it. Show how it works. Ask them some questions. Write or draw what they say.

Tell

1. Explain how you made your seed mover better.
2. Explain how it works.

Show

3. Model how it works.
4. Does it work better? **yes** **no**

Ask

5. Do you like the new design better?

Name: ______________________ Date: __________

Directions: Draw yourself as an engineer. Show how you tested your design.

Talk About It!

How well would your design work in nature?
What surprised you about the challenge?

Earth's Resources Teaching Support

Overview of Unit Activities

Students will learn about and explore Earth's resources through the following activities:

- reading about and studying pictures of natural resources
- reading about and studying pictures of renewable and nonrenewable resources
- looking for and recording natural resources around them and describing how they are used
- making leaf rubbings
- analyzing a graph of renewable and nonrenewable energy
- building water filtration systems

Materials Per Group

Week 1

- leaves (2–3)

STEAM Challenge

- basic school supplies
- coffee filters (5–10)
- dirty water (1 cup, 250 mL; see Setup and Instructional Tips)
- filter materials, such as soil, gravel, stones, dirt, cotton balls, sand (1 handful of each)
- large plastic bottle, cut in half (1)
- paper towels (5–10 sheets)

Setup and Instructional Tips

- It is recommended that students complete this challenge in partners or small groups for support.
- **Week 1 Day 4:** Giving students large sheets of paper will encourage them to include more leaf rubbings and make for more interesting final products.
- **Week 2 Day 1:** Read this challenge introduction to students. "Water is a natural resource that is very important. Plants and animals need clean water. People need clean water to drink. In this challenge, you will design a way to clean water with a water filter." Explain the challenge, the criteria, and the constraint.
- **Week 2 Day 2:** Show students the filter materials they will have available to them.
- **Testing Days:** Prepare the dirty water using crushed leaves, dirt, oil, and coffee grounds so that it includes a variety of different-sized contaminants.

Discussion Questions

- How do people use natural resources?
- How can people reduce their impact on the land, water, and air around them?
- What is the difference between renewable and nonrenewable resources?
- Why is it important to have access to clean air, water, and land?
- Where do you see examples of water filtration systems?

Additional Notes

- **Possible Misconception:** Nonrenewable resources will never come back.
  Truth: Nonrenewable resources can come back naturally, but it takes longer than a human lifetime.
- **Possible Misconception:** People can drink water if it looks clean.
  Truth: Even if water is clear, it may not be suitable to drink. It may contain germs and other pollutants that are too small to see.
- **Possible Design Solutions:** Students might layer the biggest pieces on the bottom and smaller pieces on top; students might place coffee filters or paper towels at the bottom to support the smaller materials.

Scaffolding and Extension Suggestions

- Support students who are having trouble understanding renewable and nonrenewable resources by discussing what common household items are made of. Then, sort those into renewable and nonrenewable resources.
- Challenge students to time how long it takes the water to pass through their filtration systems. The slower, the better, because the longer it takes for water to move through the filter, the cleaner it gets.

Answer Key

Week 1 Day 1

1. B
2. A

Week 1 Day 2

1. Possible answers: oil, rocks, coal, natural gas
2. Possible answers: plants, animals, sunlight, wind

Week 1 Day 3

Natural Resources: wood, cotton, leather, paper, water, food, plastic, bricks, metals, or anything made from plants

Week 1 Day 5

1. nonrenewable
2. Answers may include wind, water, or solar energy.

Weeks 2 & 3

See STEAM Challenge Rubric on page 221.

Name: ______________________ Date: __________

Directions: Read the text. Answer the questions.

Natural Resources

We get many things from nature. They are not made by people. Water and rocks are from nature. Plants and air are from nature.

1. A natural resource is made by __________ .

(A) people

(B) nature

2. A __________ is an example of a natural resource.

(A) tree

(B) car

Name: ______________________ Date: ____________

Directions: Read the text. Look at the pictures. Answer the questions.

Some things from nature take a long time to grow or form. Some things from nature can run out. They are nonrenewable. Some things from nature will never run out. Or they come back fast. They are renewable.

Nonrenewable		Renewable	
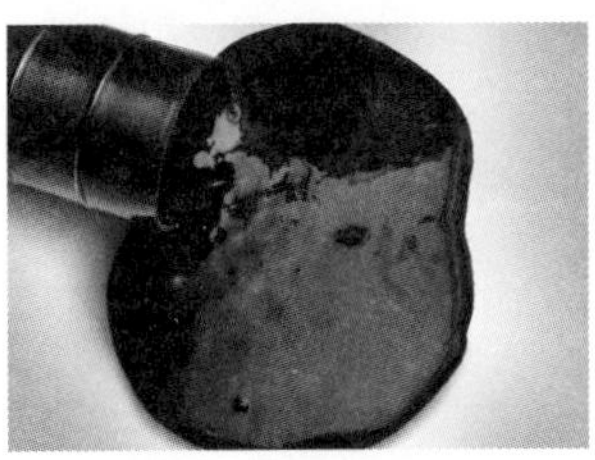 oil	 rocks	 plants	 animals
 coal	 natural gas	 sunlight	 wind

1. What is one example of a nonrenewable resource?

____

2. What is one example of a renewable resource?

____

Name: ______________________________ Date: _____________

Directions: Look around you. Go for a walk outside. Draw or write examples of natural resources. Write or draw how we use them.

Natural Resources I See	How We Use Them
 wood	 pencil

Name: ______________________ Date: __________

Directions: Collect some leaves. Look for all different shapes and sizes. Then, make a leaf rubbing. Follow the steps.

How to Make a Leaf Rubbing

1. Place a leaf upside down on a table.

2. Place a sheet of paper over the leaf.

3. Hold the paper with one hand. Rub the side of a crayon across the leaf.

4. Repeat with a new leaf and a new color.

Name: ______________________ Date: __________

Directions: Read the text. Study the pie chart. Answer the questions.

We get energy from nature. Some is from renewable resources. Some is from nonrenewable resources.

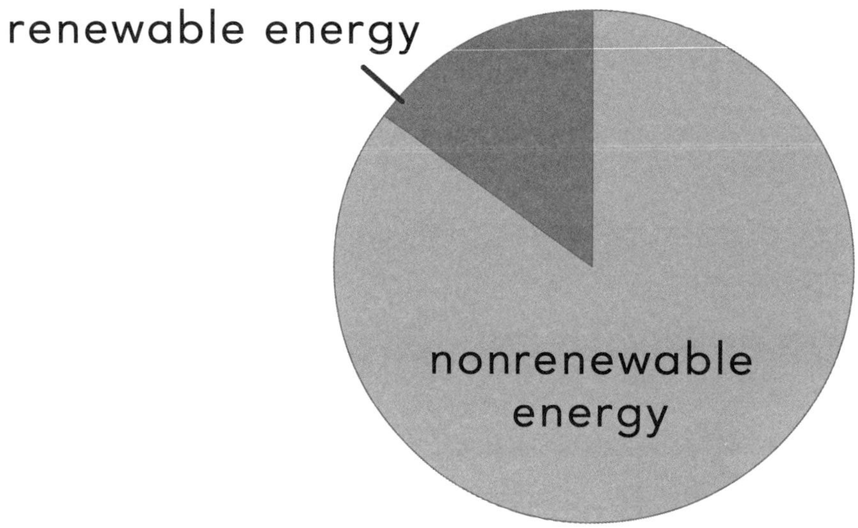

1. What type of energy is used the most?

____

2. Draw one type of renewable energy.

Name: ______________________________ Date: ____________

Directions: Read the text. Look at the picture.

The Challenge

Build a water filter.

- **Criteria**—It must make dirty water cleaner and clearer.
- **Constraint**—You may use only the materials given to you.

Filter Setup

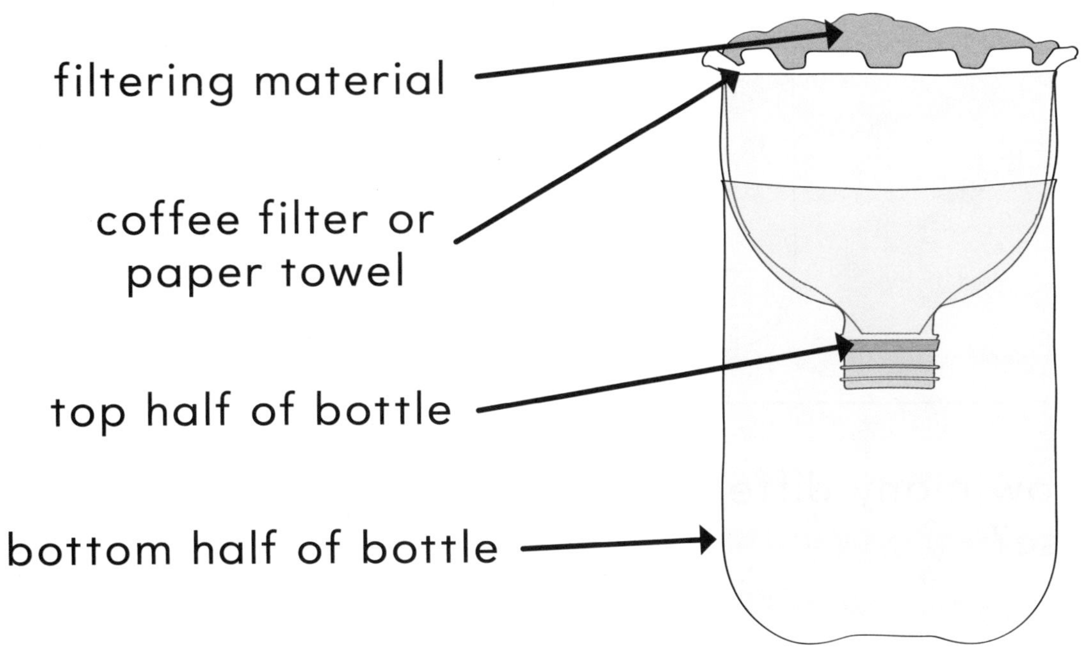

Talk About It!

What are some questions you have about the challenge?

Think About It!

What are some things you could use to help filter the water?

Name: ______________________ Date: __________

Directions: Read the text. Answer the questions.

How Does a Water Filter Work?

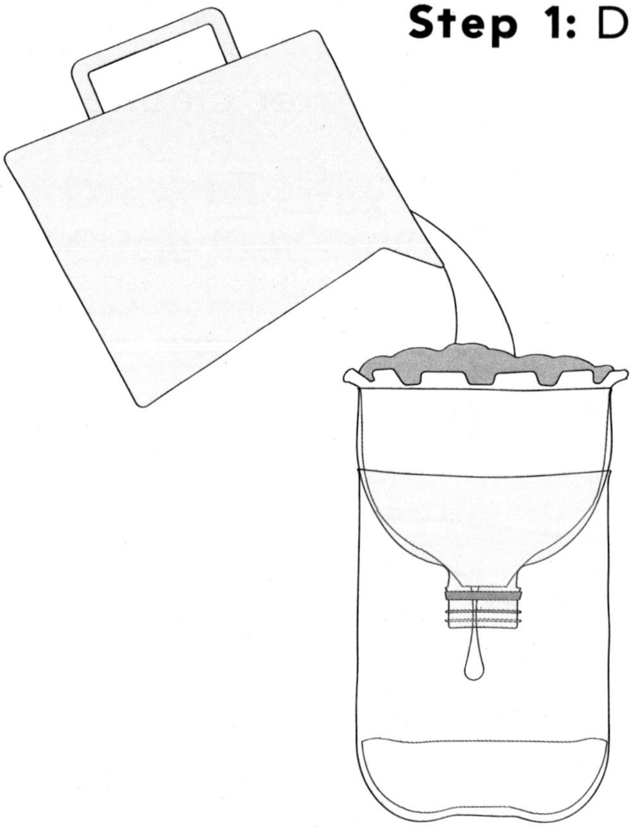

Step 1: Dirty water goes in.

Step 2: Dirt and other things get stuck in the filter.

Step 3: Clean water comes out of the bottom.

1. How many different filtering materials will you use?

   2 3 4 5

2. What will you put in first?

   ____

Name: ______________________ Date: ____________

Directions: Sketch your filter. Show where the materials will go. Label the materials in your filter.

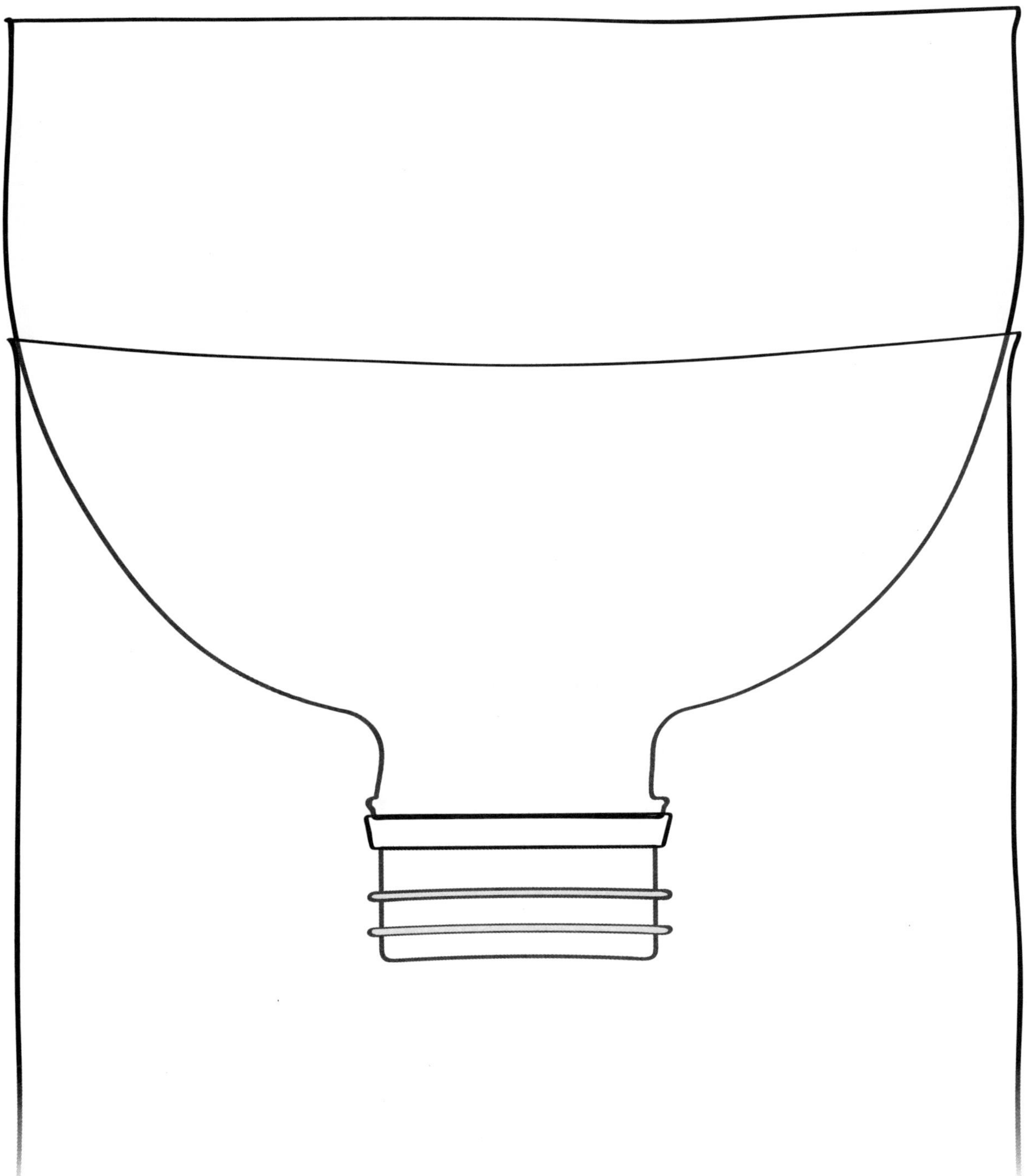

Name: ______________________ Date: ____________

Directions: Build your water filter. Check off the steps as you go.

- [ ] Look at your design sketch.
- [ ] Gather the materials you need.
- [ ] Put the bottom half of the bottle on the table.
- [ ] Place the upside-down top inside.
- [ ] Rest a coffee filter inside.
- [ ] Layer your filtering materials.

Quick Tip!

If something is not working, try different materials!

Name: ______________________________ Date: ____________

Directions: Draw the dirty water. Pour dirty water into your filter. Wait as it drips through to the bottom. Draw the water again.

Dirty Water	Filtered Water

Name: ______________________ Date: ____________

Directions: Think about your water filter design. Answer the questions.

1. How well did your filter clean the water?

2. Draw two filter designs that you saw from others. Show the materials.

Design 1	**Design 2**

Name: ______________________ Date: ____________

Directions: Plan your new design. Then, sketch your new design.

1. Will you change how many layers of material you have?

   yes **no**

2. Will you change or add materials?

   yes **no**

3. Will you change the order of your layers?

   yes **no**

Name: ______________________________ Date: ____________

Directions: Rebuild your water filter. Check off the steps as you go.

- [ ] Look at your design sketch.
- [ ] Gather the materials you need.
- [ ] Put the bottom half of the bottle on the table.
- [ ] Place the upside-down top inside.
- [ ] Rest a coffee filter inside.
- [ ] Layer your filtering materials.

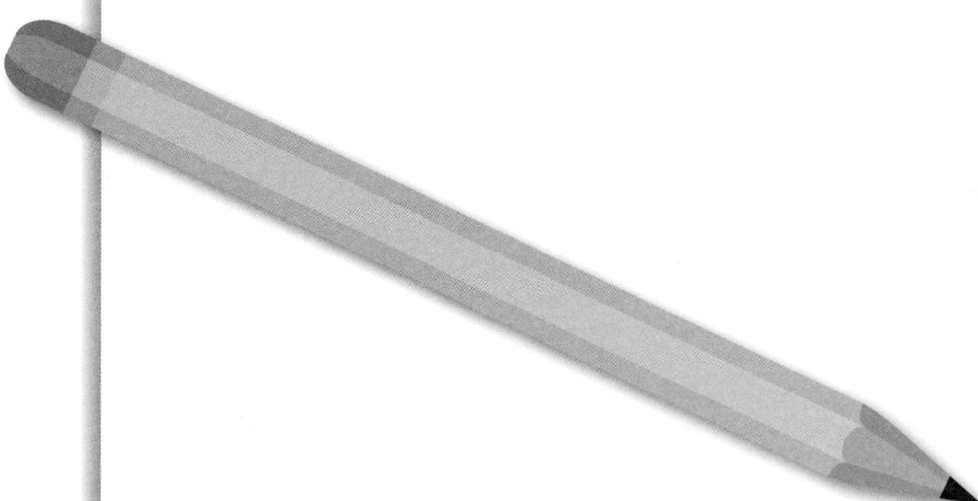

Name: ______________________________ Date: ____________

Directions: Draw the dirty water. Pour dirty water into your filter. Wait as it drips through to the bottom. Draw the water again. Answer the question.

Dirty Water	Filtered Water

1. Did it work better?

yes **no**

Name: ______________________________ Date: ____________

Directions: Draw yourself as an engineer. Show how you worked to build your filter.

Talk About It!

What part of your design are you most proud of? What filtering materials worked well?

Reduce, Reuse, Recycle Teaching Support

Overview of Unit Activities

Students will learn about and explore how to reduce, reuse, and recycle through the following activities:

- reading about and studying pictures that explain how things can be recycled
- reading about the differences between reducing, reusing, and recycling
- sorting recyclable and nonrecyclable materials
- designing smaller packaging to reduce waste
- analyzing a graph showing how many items are recycled
- planning and making recycled paper

Materials Per Group

- basic school supplies
- blender (1)
- cookie cutter (1)
- food coloring and/or flower petals (optional additions to paper recipes)
- small bowl or cup (1)
- spoon (1)
- various types of paper (newspaper, copy paper, magazines, wrapping paper, greeting cards, cardboard, etc.)
- woven wire mesh screen or an old screen from a window (1)

Setup and Instructional Tips

- **Week 2 Day 1:** Read this challenge introduction to students. "Paper is made from fibers. Most of the time, the fibers come from trees. But paper can also be made from other things. It can be made from other used paper. You will write a recipe for paper using recycled things. Then, you will make your paper and test it." Explain the challenge, the criteria, and the constraint.
- **Week 2 Day 3:** Read the recipe information to students. "You will make paper the size of cookie cutters (show them). Each small sheet of paper you make will have 5 spoonfuls of fiber mixed with water. You can use more than one spoonful of each thing. What will you use in your recipe?" Show students the materials they will be able to use. Have them write their recipes.

- **Making Recycled Paper Tips:** Prior to building days, have students sort recycled paper into types, rip the paper into small pieces, and soak for at least two hours. Using spoons, students will make their mixtures according to their "recipes" in bowls. After soaking, and just prior to making the paper, an adult will blend the mix it into a smooth, pulpy texture. You may need to add more water as you blend. Have each child press the pulp into the cookie cutters placed atop the mesh screen and push to flatten the paper and squeeze out the excess water. Allow about 24 hours for the paper to dry before removing the cookie cutter and carefully peeling it off the screen.
- **Safety Note:** An adult should operate the blender.

Discussion Questions

- What choices can people make to reduce their impact on the land, water, air, and living things?
- How do people affect the world around them?
- Why is it important for people to reduce, reuse, and recycle?
- How do you reduce, reuse, or recycle at home or school?
- Where do you see other examples of reducing, reusing, and recycling around you?

Additional Notes

- **Possible Misconception:** All items in the trash can be recycled.
  Truth: Only some items we commonly throw away can be recycled.
- **Possible Student Design Solutions:** Students may try different materials in different amounts. Students may try to use only one material or may use two or more.

Scaffolding and Extension Suggestions

- Support students to understand how materials are recycled by showing them pictures or videos of recycling plants that show how materials are recycled.
- Challenge students to more accurately measure the recycled materials in their "recipes" by teaching them how to gently level off the spoons.

Answer Key

Week 1 Day 1

1. B
2. A

Week 1 Day 2

1. reduce, reuse, recycle
2. Answers should show that recycling is when you make something new from something old.

Week 1 Day 3

Can Be Recycled: plastic bottle, glass bottle, can, newspaper, soda can

Cannot Be Recycled: broken glass, foam plate, foam cup

Week 1 Day 5

1. paper
2. 2
3. cardboard boxes

Weeks 2 & 3

See STEAM Challenge Rubric on page 221.

Name: ______________________________ Date: ____________

Directions: Read the text. Look at the pictures. Answer the questions.

What happens to a plastic bottle when you are done with it? That depends on you. You can throw it in the trash. Then, it will go to a landfill. Landfills can fill up. They can also harm plants and animals nearby. Or you can recycle it. It can be made into something new. A stuffed toy can be made from recycled bottles.

1. Which best tells about a landfill?

   (A) It is good for plants and animals.

   (B) It can harm plants and animals.

2. What can be made from recycled bottles?

   (A) a stuffed toy

   (B) a paper plate

Name: ______________________ Date: ____________

Directions: Read the text. Answer the questions.

The Three Rs

The three Rs help keep Earth clean. When you **reduce**, you make less trash. When you **reuse**, you find new ways to use things. When you **recycle**, you make new things from old things.

1. Name the three Rs.

2. Write or draw what it means to recycle.

Name: ______________________________ Date: ____________

Directions: Read the text. Then, sort the recycling. Circle plastic items. Draw an *X* over glass items.

Recycle

Things must be sorted to be recycled. Glass goes in one pile. Paper and cardboard go in another. Metal goes in a third pile. Plastic things are sorted, too.

Name: ______________________ Date: ____________

Directions: Read the text. Draw a new, smaller package for food.

Reduce

People can reduce what they use. This means they can use less stuff. A company can reduce, too. They can make packages smaller. Think of a food you eat a lot. How can you redesign the package to make it smaller?

Name: ______________________________ Date: ____________

Directions: Read the text. Study the chart. Answer the questions.

Ishar helped his mom recycle. They recycled these items from their house.

Item	Amount
plastic bottles	
sheets of paper	
glass bottles	
cardboard boxes	

1. What item did they recycle the most of?

____

2. How many glass bottles did they recycle? ________

3. Which item did they recycle four of?

____

Name: ______________________________ Date: ____________

Directions: Read the text. Then, look at the materials. Circle the things you think you can use to make paper.

The Challenge

Plan a recipe for recycled paper. Follow the recipe to make recycled paper.

- **Criteria**—The paper must stay together.
- **Constraint**—You must use paper materials.

newspaper

plastic bottles

tissue paper

glass jars

cardboard

tin cans

magazines

office paper

aluminum cans

Name: ______________________ Date: __________

Directions: Read the text. Study the diagram. Then, answer the question.

Paper has been made the same way for a long, long time. Water and fibers from trees are used. They are made into mushy pulp. Chemicals are added. The pulp is poured into a filter. The water drains away. The filtered pulp dries. Then, the paper is rolled out.

How Paper Is Made

Bark is removed.

Wood is cut.

Water is added.

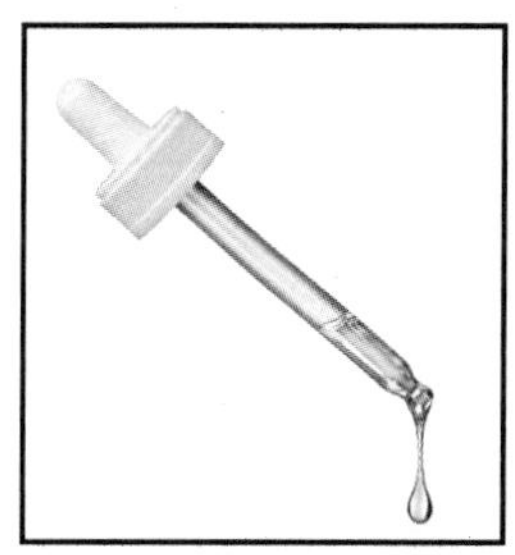

Chemicals are added. It is filtered.

It is put on rolls.

1. What will you use to make recycled paper? Write three things.

____

____

____

Name: ______________________ Date: ____________

Directions: Plan your recipe. You will use five spoonfuls of material. Write what materials you will use.

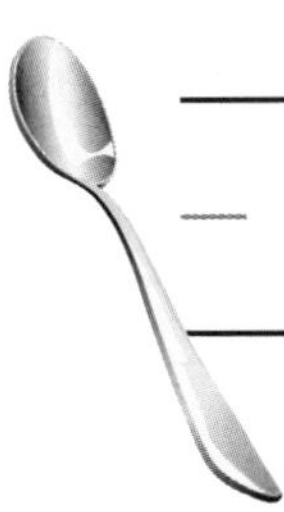

Name: ______________________________ Date: ____________

Directions: Make your recycled paper. Check off the steps as you go.

- ☐ Look at your recipe.
- ☐ Gather the materials you need.
- ☐ Measure your ingredients.
- ☐ Ask an adult to blend it into pulp.
- ☐ Place your cookie cutter on top of the mesh.
- ☐ Pour the paper pulp into the cookie cutter.
- ☐ Push the pulp with your fingers to flatten it and get out the extra water.
- ☐ Let it dry.

Quick Tip!

Leave the cookie cutter in place until the paper dries.

Name: ______________________________ Date: ____________

Directions: Read the text. Then, slowly lift the cookie cutter. Peel the paper off the screen. Look at and feel your paper. Answer the questions.

The paper you made is different from paper made in factories. It is smaller and a bit bumpy. But it is still paper. It is okay if your paper does not look like normal paper.

1. How does your paper look? Draw it.

2. How does your paper feel?

____

____

3. Write on your paper. Does it work?

yes **no** **a little**

Name: ______________________ Date: ____________

Directions: Read the text. Think about your recycled paper. Answer the questions.

1. How well did your recipe work?

2. Do you want to take out any ingredients?

   yes **no**

3. Do you want to add any ingredients?

   yes **no**

4. Draw two pieces of recycled paper that you saw from others.

Recycled Paper 1	Recycled Paper 2

Name: ______________________________ Date: ____________

Directions: Plan your new recipe. Write your ingredients. Circle any changes you made.

Name: ______________________________ Date: ____________

Directions: Make your new paper recipe. Check off the steps as you go.

- ☐ Look at your recipe.
- ☐ Gather the materials you need.
- ☐ Measure your ingredients.
- ☐ Ask your teacher to blend it into pulp.
- ☐ Place your cookie cutter on top of the mesh.
- ☐ Pour the paper pulp into the cookie cutter.
- ☐ Push the pulp with your fingers to flatten it and get out the extra water.
- ☐ Let it dry.

Name: ______________________ Date: ____________

Directions: Slowly lift the cookie cutter. Peel the paper off the screen. Look, touch, and feel your paper. Answer the questions.

1. How do you feel about your new recipe?

2. Is it better than your first recipe? Why or why not?

3. What does your new paper look like? Draw it.

Name: ______________________ Date: ____________

Directions: Draw different ways you can use your paper.

Talk About It!

What part of your recipe are you most proud of? What did you learn from this challenge?

Severe Weather Teaching Support

Overview of Unit Activities

Students will learn about and explore severe weather through the following activities:

- reading about severe weather
- reading about severe weather forecasting
- making tornados in bottles
- painting rainbows
- analyzing a five-day forecast
- building umbrellas to protect toys from rain

Materials Per Group

Week 1

- construction paper (1 sheet)
- dish soap
- empty water bottle with lid (1)
- glitter (1 spoonful)
- paint (colors of the rainbow)
- paintbrush (1)

STEAM Challenge

- basic school supplies
- colander (1)
- craft sticks (2–3)
- fabric pieces (6; 5" x 5" each, or 13 cm x 13 cm each)
- foil (2 feet, 60 cm)
- large plastic tub (1)
- paper plates (2)
- pipe cleaners (5)
- plastic cups (2)
- plastic wrap (2 feet, 60 cm)
- ruler (1)
- small toy (1)
- sponges (1–2)
- water (1 cup, 250 mL)

Setup and Instructional Tips

- **Week 2 Day 1:** Read this challenge introduction to students. "Have you ever used an umbrella? It probably kept you dry from the rain. In this challenge, you will build an umbrella to protect a toy from getting wet." Explain the challenge, the criteria, and the constraint.
- **Testing Days:** Have student groups take turns placing the toy under their umbrellas and pouring water though a colander to simulate rain.
- Be mindful that some students may get nervous talking about severe weather. Focus on how people can prepare and respond to it to stay safe.

Discussion Questions

- What are some examples of extreme weather?
- How can we prepare for extreme weather?
- What kinds of severe weather are common where we live?
- Why is it important to prepare and respond to extreme weather events?
- How does weather affect people's day-to-day lives?

Additional Notes

- **Possible Misconception:** Snow and ice make it cold.
  Truth: Snow and ice are the result of cold temperatures, not the cause.
- **Possible Student Design Solutions:** Students may build umbrellas that open and close, that are flat or curved, or umbrellas with multiple shafts.

Scaffolding and Extension Suggestions

- Support students with understanding the difference between typical weather and severe weather by talking about the frequency of occurrence.
- Challenge students who built successful umbrellas during the first design to protect larger toys from the rain.

Answer Key

Week 1 Day 1

1. B
2. B

Week 1 Day 2

1. weather tools
2. get ready
3. Responses should include something to prepare for a storm, such as dressing warm, going inside, or stocking up on food.

Week 1 Day 3

Drawings should show vortexes of water and glitter inside bottles.

Week 1 Day 5

1. Sunday, Monday, Wednesday
2. partly cloudy
3. Monday

Weeks 2 & 3

See STEAM Challenge Rubric on page 221.

Name: ______________________________ Date: ____________

Directions: Read the text. Answer the questions.

Severe Weather

Have you ever seen lightning? Storms are one type of severe weather. Floods, tornados, and hail are other types. Severe weather does not happen often. But when it does, there are things you can do to stay safe.

When thunder roars, go indoors!

1. What is one type of severe weather?

   (A) rain

   (B) flood

2. What is one thing people can do to stay safe in severe weather?

   (A) watch the lightning

   (B) go inside

Name: ______________________ Date: __________

Directions: Read the text. Answer the questions.

Weather Forecasting

Weather scientists are helpful. They can tell us when severe weather is coming. They use weather tools. These tools help them know when severe weather is coming. This gives people time to plan. It helps people get ready. It helps keep people safe.

1. What do weather scientists use to help them predict a storm is coming?

____

2. Knowing when severe weather is coming helps ______________________ people ______________________.

3. Draw how you might prepare for a storm.

Name: ______________________ Date: ____________

Directions: Follow the steps to make a tornado in a bottle. Check off the steps as you go. Then, draw what you saw.

- ☐ Fill your bottle $\frac{3}{4}$ of the way full with clean water.
- ☐ Add a squirt of dish soap.
- ☐ Add a spoonful of glitter.
- ☐ Tighten the lid.
- ☐ Quickly move the bottle in circles. The water should begin swirling.
- ☐ Watch your tornado!

Talk About It!

What types of damage could a real tornado do?

Name: ______________________________ Date: ____________

Directions: Rainbows can come after storms. Make your own rainbow. Check off the steps as you go.

- ☐ Draw two fluffy clouds on opposite sides of a sheet of paper.

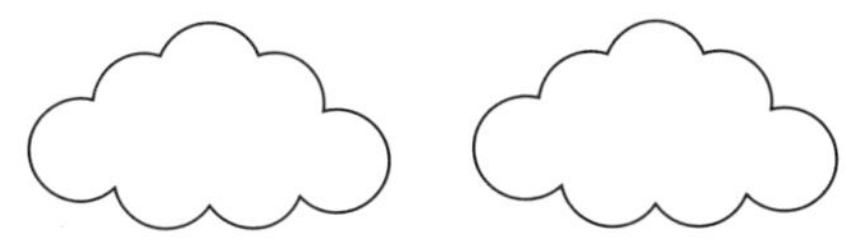

- ☐ Draw a small curve connecting the clouds.

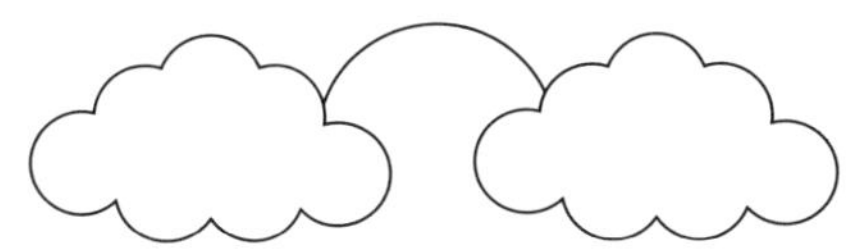

- ☐ Draw another curve about a finger above.

- ☐ Repeat until you have made six stripes.
- ☐ Using red paint, trace over the top stripe from cloud to cloud.

- ☐ Do one for each color of the rainbow: red, orange, yellow, green, blue, and purple.
- ☐ Paint the clouds white.
- ☐ Let your painting dry.

Name: ______________________ Date: ____________

Directions: Look at the weather forecast. Answer the questions.

5-Day Forecast				
Sunday	**Monday**	**Tuesday**	**Wednesday**	**Thursday**
 snow	 blizzard warning	 partly cloudy	 snow	 sunny

1. Which days will it likely snow?

____

____

____

2. What will the weather be like on Tuesday?

____

3. On which day could there be severe weather?

____

Name: ______________________ Date: ____________

Directions: Read the text. Then, draw a time you used an umbrella.

The Challenge

Make an umbrella to protect a toy from rain.

- **Criteria**—It must keep the toy dry when water is poured on it.
- **Constraint**—You may use only the materials given to you.

Name: ______________________ Date: __________

Directions: Look at the parts of an umbrella. Answer the questions.

1. What parts will you change?

____

____

2. How big will your umbrella need to be to keep your toy dry?

__________ inches

Talk About It!

What other ideas do you have for your umbrella?

Name: ______________________ Date: __________

Directions: Sketch your umbrella. Label the parts of your umbrella.

Think About It!

What materials will work best to keep the toy dry?

Name: ______________________________ Date: ____________

Directions: Build your umbrella. Check off the steps as you go.

- ☐ Look at your design sketch.
- ☐ Gather the materials you need.
- ☐ Build the parts of your umbrella.
- ☐ Attach them together.
- ☐ Check that all parts are glued or taped well.

Name: ______________________________ Date: ____________

Directions: Place your toy in a tub. Hold your umbrella over it. Have a friend hold a colander over your umbrella. Have them pour some water into the colander. Check how dry your toy is. Answer the questions.

1. Is the toy dry?

   yes **no**

2. Is the umbrella dry?

   yes **no**

3. Did the umbrella fall apart?

   yes **no**

4. Could you use the umbrella again?

   yes **no**

Name: ______________________________ Date: _____________

Directions: Think about your umbrella design. Answer the questions.

1. How well did your umbrella work?

2. Would you use it in the rain?

yes **no**

3. Draw two umbrella designs you saw from others. Put a checkmark by the one that worked the best.

☐ **Design 1**	☐ **Design 2**

Name: ______________________ Date: ____________

Directions: Plan your new design. Then, sketch your new design.

1. What parts will you change?

____

____

2. Do you need to change the size of your umbrella?

yes **no**

Name: ______________________ Date: ____________

Directions: Rebuild your umbrella. Check off the steps as you go.

- ☐ Look at your new design sketch.
- ☐ Tell a friend why this new design will make it better.
- ☐ Gather the materials you need.
- ☐ Rebuild your umbrella. Make the changes you want.
- ☐ Check that all parts are glued or taped well.

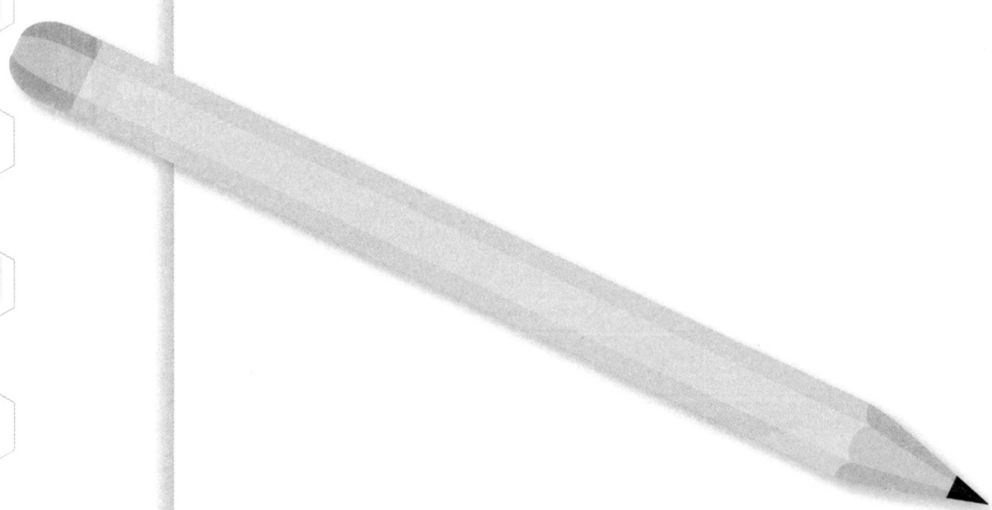

Name: ______________________________ Date: ____________

Directions: Place your toy in a tub. Hold your umbrella over it. Have a friend hold a colander over your umbrella. Have them pour some water into the colander. Check how dry your toy is. Answer the questions.

1. Is the toy dry?

   yes **no**

2. Is the umbrella dry?

   yes **no**

3. Did the umbrella fall apart?

   yes **no**

4. Could you use the umbrella again?

   yes **no**

5. Did the new design work better?

   yes **no**

Name: ______________________ Date: __________

Directions: Draw a friend using your umbrella on a rainy day.

Talk About It!

What part of your design are you most proud of?
What did you learn from this challenge?

Warmth from the Sun Teaching Support

Overview of Unit Activities

Students will learn about and explore how sunlight warms Earth through the following activities:

- reading about and studying pictures of sunlight hitting Earth
- reading about heat given off by the sun
- experimenting with ice cubes in the sun and shade
- creating paintings with daytime and nighttime colors
- analyzing data of sunlight hours in different seasons
- building shade structures

Materials Per Group

Week 1

- ice cubes
- paint
- paintbrushes

STEAM Challenge

- basic school supplies
- construction paper (2 sheets)
- craft sticks (10+)
- masking tape
- rock (1)
- thick and thin pieces of fabric (4–5 pieces)
- tissue paper (2 pieces)

Setup and Instructional Tips

- **Week 2 Day 1:** Read this challenge introduction to students. "The sun shines on everything around us. The sun gives off heat. It makes us hot. Shade is an area that is blocked from getting direct sunlight. Because shade blocks the sunlight, it is cooler. A tree can provide shade. So can an umbrella. You will build a structure to provide shade." Explain the challenge, the criteria, and the constraint.
- **Testing Days:** When testing shade structures, place them in open areas where they will receive direct sunlight in the morning, midday, and afternoon. Students will need to check their designs in the morning, midday, and afternoon.

Discussion Questions

- What is sunlight? When do you see it?
- When have you used shade to protect yourself from the sun?
- How can you tell if a surface is hotter than another?
- What types of shade are better than others?
- How and when does sunlight warm Earth's surface?
- What happens when an ice cube is left in the sun?

Additional Notes

- **Possible Misconception:** The sun isn't out on cloudy days.
  Truth: The sun is still in the sky, but the clouds are too thick for the same amount of light to get through.
- **Possible Student Design Solutions:** Students might build shade structures that are flat and only block the sun from directly above. Encourage them to consider the apparent movement of the sun.

Scaffolding and Extension Suggestions

- Support students with understanding the challenge by discussing where the sun will be in the sky in the morning, midday, and afternoon.
- Challenge students by placing ice cubes in the sun and under each shade structure. Compare how long it takes for the ice cubes to melt.

Answer Key

Week 1 Day 1

1. A
2. A

Week 1 Day 2

1. the sun
2. Responses may include land, water, air, or anything warmed by the sun.
3. Drawings should include something being warmed by sunlight.

Week 1 Day 3

Drawings should show ice melting faster in the sun and slower in the shade.

Week 1 Day 5

1. summer
2. winter
3. 12

Weeks 2 & 3

See STEAM Challenge Rubric on page 221.

Name: ______________________ Date: __________

Directions: Read the text. Answer the questions.

Sunlight

The sun shines. This means it gives off light. The light makes it bright during the day. Earth spins. When it turns away from the sun, it is night. It is dark at night.

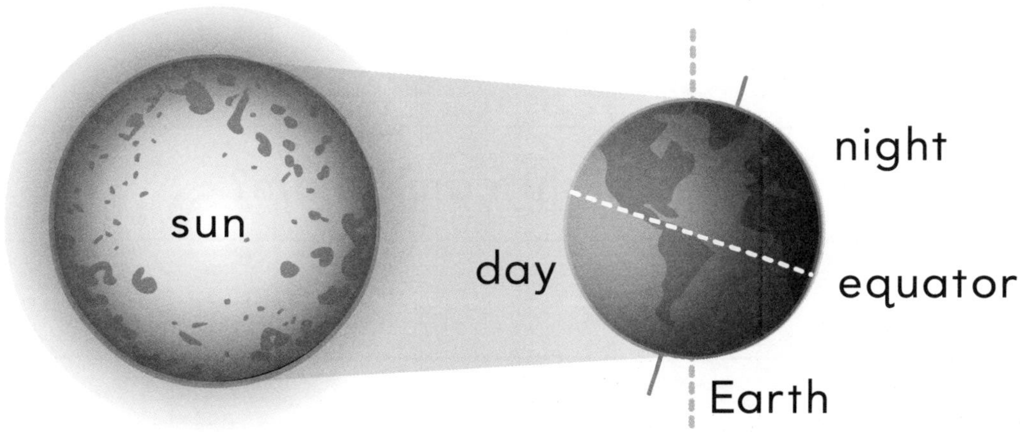

1. When do you see sunshine?

   (A) during the day

   (B) at night

2. What does the light do?

   (A) makes it bright

   (B) makes it dark

Name: ______________________ Date: __________

Directions: Read the text. Answer the questions.

Light from the sun warms Earth. This is called *sunlight*. It warms the land. It warms the water. It warms the air. This is why things are warmer when they are in the sun.

1. Where does sunlight come from?

____

2. What is something that is warmed by sunlight?

____

3. Draw something being warmed by sunlight.

Name: ______________________ Date: __________

Directions: Place one ice cube in the sun. Place another in the shade. Draw the ice cubes. Wait a few minutes. Draw them again.

At First

In the Sunlight	In the Shade

After a Few Minutes

In the Sunlight	In the Shade

Name: ______________________ Date: ____________

Directions: Make a day and night painting. Check off the items as you go.

- ☐ Fold a large sheet of white paper in half.
- ☐ Use a black marker. Draw a line down the middle.
- ☐ Choose a side to be day. Use warm colors to paint the sunlight.
- ☐ On the other side, use cool colors to paint the nighttime sky.
- ☐ Stand back, and look at what you made.

Warm Colors	**Cool Colors**
red	green
orange	blue
yellow	purple

Name: ______________________ Date: ____________

Directions: Read the text. Look at the chart. Answer the questions.

Daylight hours change as the seasons change. Noah and his mom wrote how long the sun was out each season. Here is what they wrote.

Daylight Hours	
Winter (January)	10
Spring (April)	12
Summer (July)	14
Fall (October)	12

1. Which season has the most hours of daylight?

____

2. Which season has the fewest hours of daylight?

____

3. How many hours of daylight were there in October?

____

Name: ______________________________ Date: ____________

Directions: Read the text. Then, label the picture.

The Challenge

Make a shade structure that protects a rock from the sun.

- **Criteria**—It should give shade in the morning, midday, and afternoon.
- **Constraint**—You may use only fabric, paper, craft sticks, and tape.

Word Bank

shade sun sunlight

Name: ______________________________ Date: ____________

Directions: Read the questions. Circle the options you like. Answer the questions.

1. What shape will you make your structure?

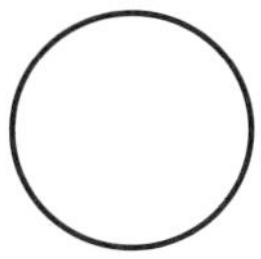
circle

square

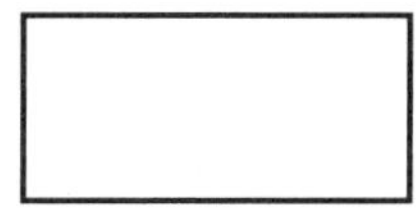
rectangle

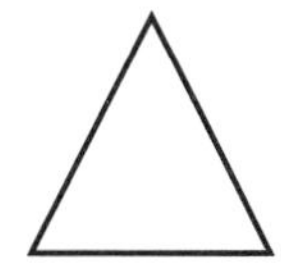
triangle

2. What will it be made of?

paper

fabric

both

3. How will your structure stay up? Draw some ideas.

Name: ______________________________ Date: ____________

Directions: Sketch your shade structure. Label the parts.

Word Bank

craft stick	fabric	paper	tape

Name: ______________________________ Date: ____________

Directions: Build your shade structure. Check off the steps as you go.

- ☐ Look at your design sketch.
- ☐ Gather the materials you need.
- ☐ Build the top of your shade structure.
- ☐ Build the sides of your shade structure.
- ☐ Attach the top and sides.
- ☐ Check that all parts are taped well.
- ☐ Check that the structure is stable.

Quick Tip!

It is okay to change your design as you go!

Name: ______________________ Date: ____________

Directions: Put your structure in a sunny spot. Place a rock under your shade. Draw what you see three times in the same day. Answer the question.

Morning

Midday

Afternoon

1. Did it shade the rock all day?

yes **no**

Name: ______________________________ Date: ____________

Directions: Think about your shade structure. Answer the questions.

1. How well did your design work?

2. Did your structure block all the sun?

   yes **no**

3. Draw two shade designs that you saw from others. Put a checkmark by your favorite.

☐ **Design 1**	☐ **Design 2**

Talk About It!

Which materials blocked the sun best? Do thick or thin materials work better?

Name: ______________________________ Date: ____________

Directions: Plan your new design. Then, sketch your new design.

1. Will you change the shape of your structure?

   yes **no**

2. Will you change the size of your structure?

   yes **no**

3. Will you use different materials?

   yes **no**

Try This!

Be creative! See how different you can make this design.

Name: ______________________________ Date: ____________

Directions: Build your shade structure. Make it work better. Check off the steps as you go.

- ☐ Look at your design sketch.
- ☐ Look at your first shade structure.
- ☐ Tell a friend how you will make it better.
- ☐ Gather the materials you need.
- ☐ Make the changes you want.
- ☐ Check that all parts are taped well.
- ☐ Check that the structure is stable.

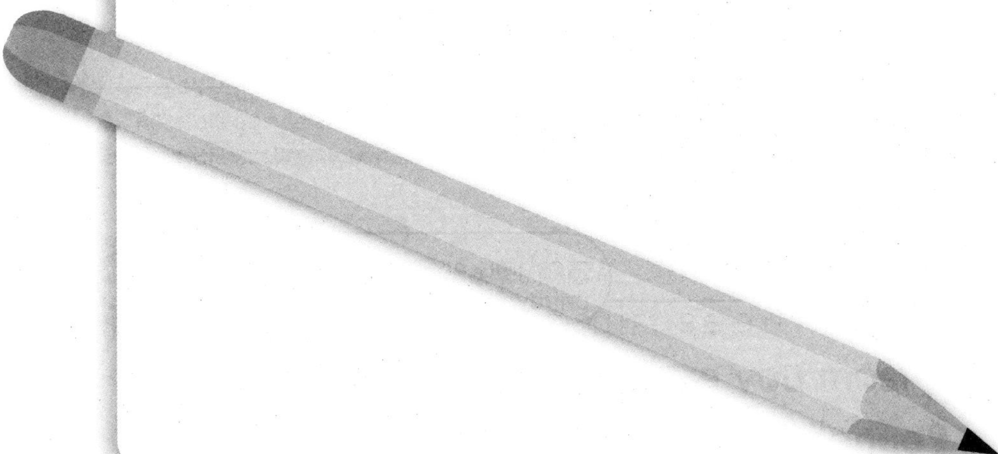

Name: ______________________ Date: ____________

Directions: Put your structure in a sunny spot. Place a rock under your shade. Draw what you see three times in the same day. Answer the questions.

Morning

Midday

Afternoon

1. Did it shade the rock all day? **yes** **no**
2. Did your structure work better this time?

   yes **no**

Name: ______________________________ Date: ____________

Directions: Draw yourself as an engineer. Show how you tested your shade structure design.

Talk About It!

What surprised you about this challenge?
What was hard about this challenge?

Wind Teaching Support

Overview of Unit Activities

Students will learn about and explore wind and weather through the following activities:

- reading about and studying pictures of weather
- reading about and studying pictures of how weather affects our lives
- making clouds in jars
- making weather wheels
- analyzing a weekly weather report
- building wind catchers

Materials Per Group

Week 1

- aerosol hair spray
- hot water (1 cup, 250 mL)
- ice
- jar with a lid (1)
- paper plate (1)
- small brad (1)

STEAM Challenge

- basic school supplies
- cardboard tubes (2–3)
- fan (1)
- paper cups in different sizes (5–6)
- plastic cups in different sizes (5–10)
- straws (2)
- wooden skewers (2)

Setup and Instructional Tips

- **Week 1 Day 3:** Adults should handle the hot water for making clouds.
- **Week 1 Day 4:** For the weather wheels, save time by punching holes in the centers of the paper plates before distributing them to students.
- **Week 2 Day 1:** Read this challenge introduction to students. "How do you measure the wind if you can't see it? A wind catcher can tell you if the wind is blowing quickly or slowly. The wind makes a wind catcher to spin, like a windmill. Your challenge is to build a wind catcher." Explain the challenge, the criteria, and the constraint. Show students pictures of different types of wind catchers or anemometers, which are used to measure wind speed.
- **Week 2 Day 2:** Show students the materials that they will be able to use before they begin drawing.
- **Safety Note:** Keep students away from the fan blades and power source.

Discussion Questions

- What is weather?
- How do we measure and track weather?
- How does the weather affect our lives?
- Why is it important for people to measure weather patterns?
- How can you measure wind?

Additional Notes

- **Possible Misconception:** Clouds are made of smoke.
  Truth: Visible clouds are made of tiny water droplets or ice crystals.
- **Possible Design Solutions:** Students may build wind catchers that spin vertically or horizontally. Students can build strong, steady bases so their wind catchers don't blow away.

Scaffolding and Extension Suggestions

- Support students in understanding how the cloud is formed in the jar. Explain that clouds form when vapor, an invisible gas, turns into tiny liquid drops floating in the air. In the activity, hair spray was added to the air to simulate dust particles. This helps the cloud form.
- Challenge students to learn about instruments used by meteorologists, such as thermometers, barometers, hygrometers, pyranometers, and rain gages.

Answer Key

Week 1 Day 1

1. B
2. A

Week 1 Day 2

1. Responses should include something you might do in the rain, such as splash in the puddles or watch the rain from inside.
2. Responses should include something you might wear in warm, sunny weather, such as shorts and T-shirts or bathing suits.

Week 1 Day 3

Drawings should include clouds forming in the jars.

Week 1 Day 5

1. 4 days
2. Friday
3. cloudy

Weeks 2 & 3

See STEAM Challenge Rubric on page 221.

Name: ____________________ Date: __________

Directions: Read the text. Answer the questions.

Weather

Weather is more than just sun and rain. It is what the sky and air are like outside. You might say it is warm and sunny. You might say it is cold and rainy. Weather can also be things such as fog and lighting.

1. Weather is what the air and sky are like ________.

   (A) inside

   (B) outside

2. ________ is NOT a type of weather.

   (A) mud

   (B) fog

Name: ______________________ Date: ____________

Directions: Read the text. Answer the questions.

Knowing about weather can be helpful. It helps us choose what to wear. You might wear a jacket if is cold and shorts if it is hot. It helps us choose what to do. You might go to the beach on a warm and sunny day. You might plant seeds if you know it is going to rain.

1. What is something you might do in the rain?

2. What is something you might wear on a warm and sunny day?

Name: ______________________ Date: ____________

Directions: Make a cloud in a jar. Follow the steps. Then, draw what happens.

How to Make a Cloud

1. Have your teacher pour hot water into a jar. Swirl it around to warm up the jar.
2. Quickly spray hair spray into the jar.
3. Turn the lid upside down. Place it on the top of the jar.
4. Put some ice cubes on top of the lid.
5. Watch what happens.

Name: ______________________ Date: __________

Directions: Make a weather wheel. Follow the steps.

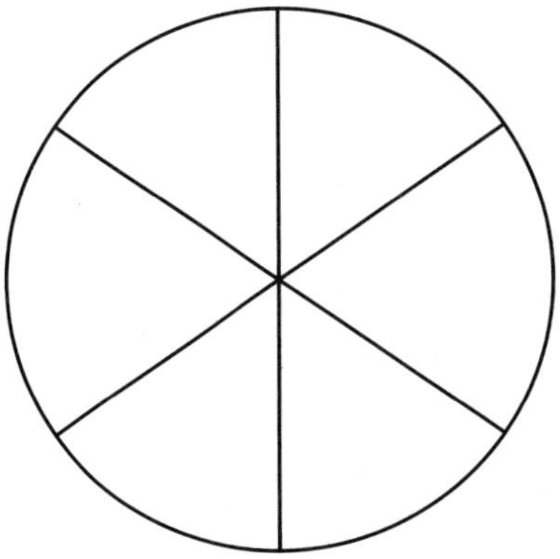

1. Draw three lines on your paper plate so it looks like a pizza.
2. Draw a type of weather in each slice. Draw: sunny, cloudy, rainy, snowy, foggy, and windy.
3. Trace out the pointer below. Cut out the pointer you traced.
4. Attach it to the center of your weather wheel. Use a brad to do this.
5. Look outside. Point the arrow to the correct weather.

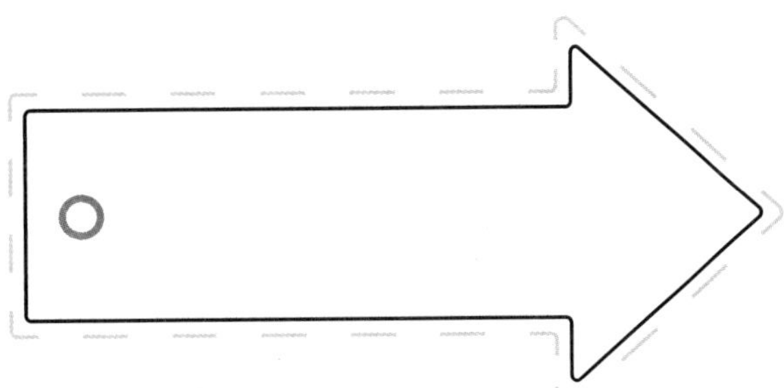

Name: ______________________________ Date: ____________

Directions: Read the text. Look at the chart. Answer the questions.

Aika tracked the weather for one week. She wrote it on the chart.

Weekly Weather Report

Monday	Tuesday	Wednesday	Thursday	Friday	Saturday	Sunday

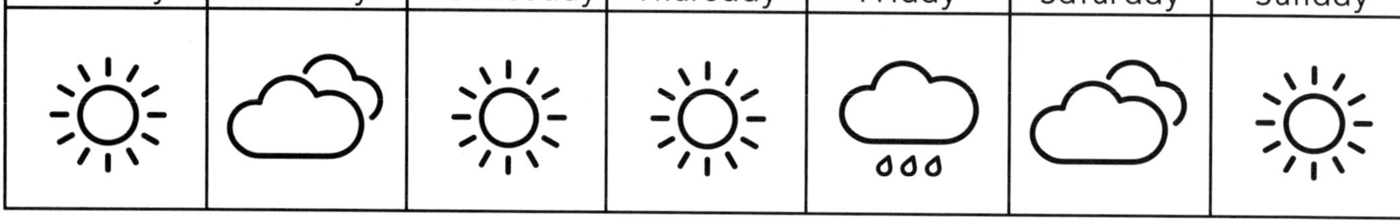

1. How many days did Aika have sunny weather?

____

2. Which day did Aika report rain?

____

3. What was the weather like on Tuesday?

____

Name: ______________________ Date: __________

Directions: Read the text. Look at the picture.

The Challenge

Make a wind catcher to measure wind speed.

- **Criteria**—It must spin faster when the wind speed increases.
- **Constraint**—You may use only the materials given to you.

Wind is moving air. It can be gentle. It can be strong. Warm air rises. Cold air moves in to take its place. This makes wind.

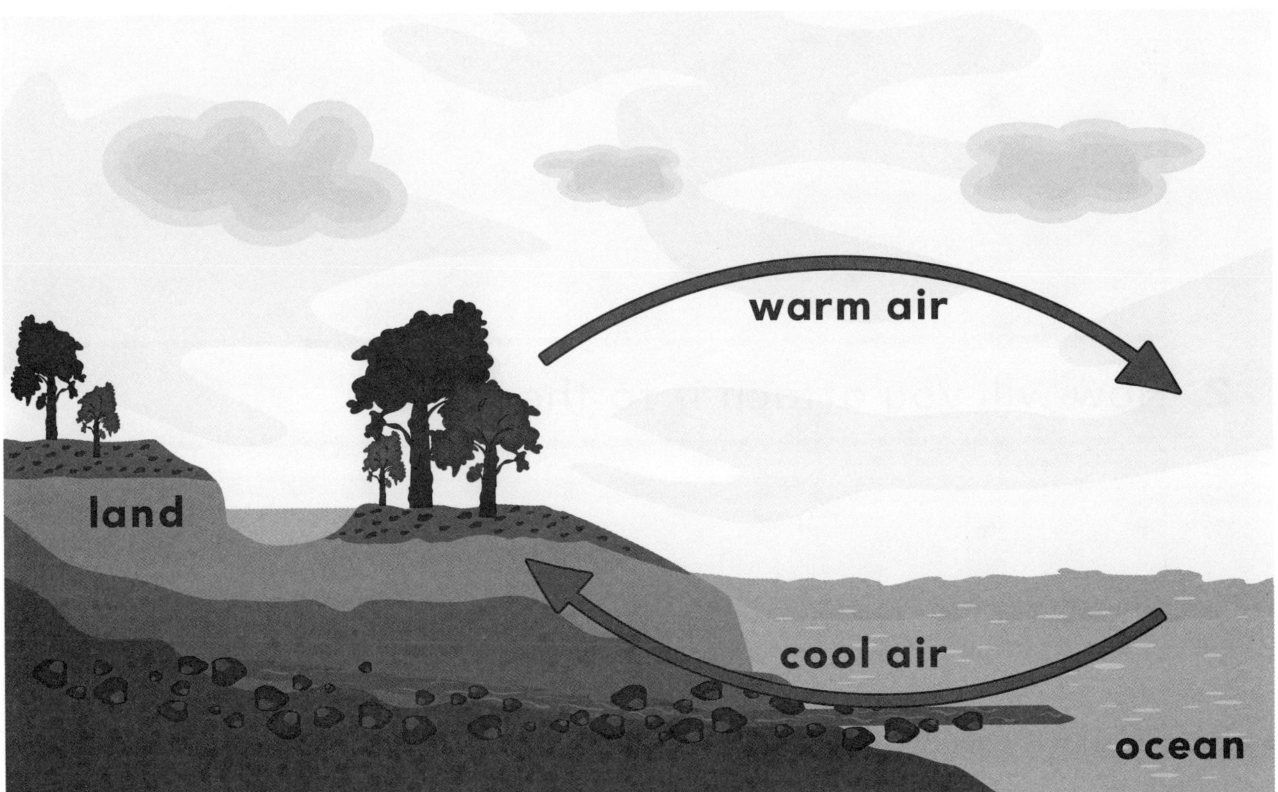

Name: ______________________ Date: ______________

Directions: Read the text. Answer the questions. Draw your answers.

This is one type of wind catcher. It moves when the wind blows.

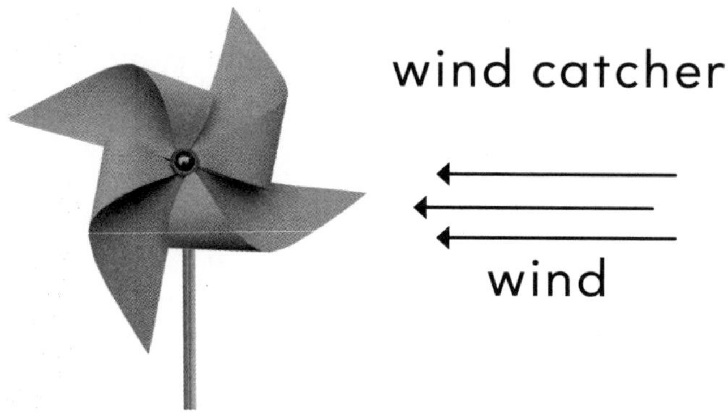

1. What will you use on the top of your wind catcher to catch the wind?

2. How will you attach it to the base?

Name: ______________________________ Date: ____________

Directions: Sketch your wind catcher. Try to draw two designs. Circle your favorite.

Name: ______________________ Date: ____________

Directions: Build your wind catcher. Check off the steps as you go.

- ☐ Look at your design sketch.
- ☐ Gather the materials you need.
- ☐ Build a solid base. This is the bottom part that helps it stand.
- ☐ Attach a pole or rod to hold your wind catcher off the ground.
- ☐ Make the spinning part.
- ☐ Attach the parts.
- ☐ Check that all parts are glued or taped well.

Name: ______________________________ Date: ____________

Directions: Set your wind catcher on the ground. Turn on a fan at low speed. Keep it on for 20 seconds. Count how many times it spins. Record it on the chart. Test your wind catcher on medium and high speed.

Fan Speed	Number of Spins
low	
medium	
high	

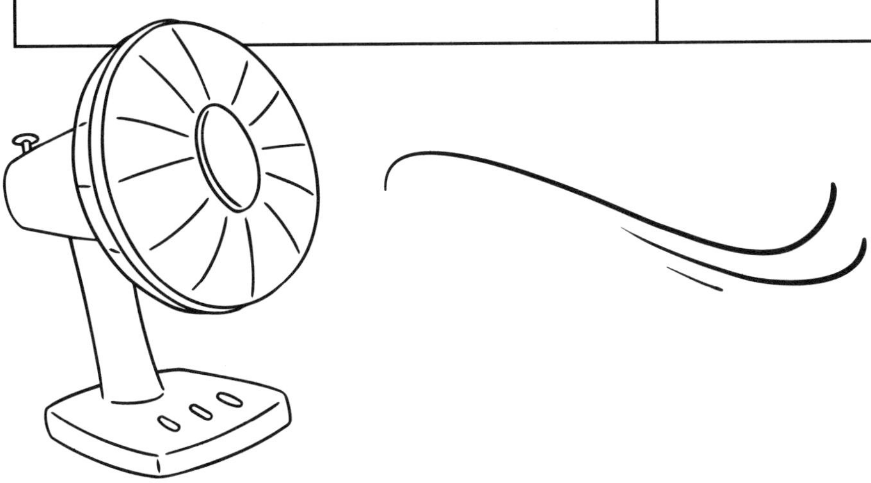

Quick Tip!

Watch as other students test their wind catchers. Notice how different wind catchers work.

Name: ______________________ Date: ____________

Directions: Think about your wind catcher design. Answer the questions.

1. How well did your wind catcher work?

2. Did it spin slower with light wind and faster with strong wind?

   yes **no**

3. Draw two wind catcher designs that you saw from other groups. Put a checkmark by the one that worked best.

☐ **Design 1**	☐ **Design 2**

Try This!

Try to find pictures of wind catchers from long ago. What do you notice?

Name: ______________________________ Date: ____________

Directions: Plan your new design. Then, sketch your new design.

1. Do you want to change your base?

   yes **no**

2. Do you want to change the shape or size of your spinning parts?

   yes **no**

3. Do you want to change the size of your pole?

   yes **no**

4. Do you want to make any other changes?

   yes **no**

Name: ______________________________ Date: ____________

Directions: Rebuild your wind catcher. Check off the steps as you go.

- ☐ Look at your new design sketch.
- ☐ Gather the materials you need.
- ☐ Rebuild a solid base.
- ☐ Rebuild and attach a pole or rod to hold your wind catcher up off the ground.
- ☐ Remake the spinning part.
- ☐ Attach it securely to the base.
- ☐ Check that all parts are glued or taped well.

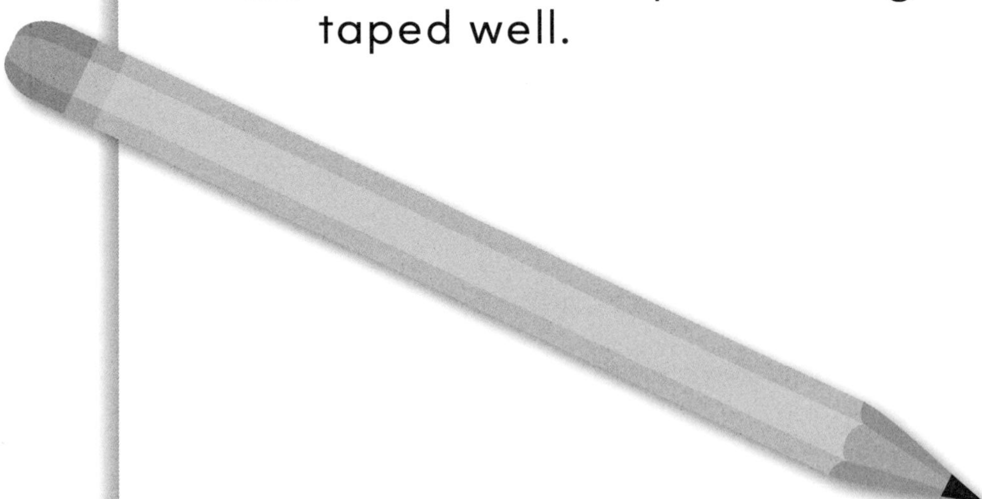

Name: ______________________ Date: ____________

Directions: Set your wind catcher on the ground. Turn on a fan at low speed. Keep it on for 20 seconds. Count how many times your wind catcher spins. Record it on the chart. Test your wind catcher on medium and high speed. Answer the questions.

Fan Speed	Number of Spins
low	
medium	
high	

1. Did your redesign work better?

yes **no**

2. How do you know?

____

____

Name: ______________________ Date: __________

Directions: Draw a windy day. Draw your wind catcher. Show how it measures wind.

Talk About It!

What part of your design are you most proud of? What was the most fun part of this challenge?

Name: ______________________________ Date: ____________

STEAM Challenge Rubric

Directions: Think about the challenge. Color in the faces to show what you did.

	Yes	A Little	Not Really
I used my materials appropriately.			
I was creative. I had new ideas.			
I worked well with others.			
I followed directions.			

Teacher Notes

____

____

____

____

Name: ______________________ Date: __________

Summative Assessment

Directions: Read the questions. Fill in the best answer.

1. What do engineers do?

- (A) build things
- (B) solve problems
- (C) A and B

2. A friend made a house for their toys. It is made of wood. It keeps falling over. What do you tell them?

- (A) Try a new material.
- (B) Have an adult fix it.
- (C) Build something else.

3. You want to build a boat. What will you do first?

- (A) test it
- (B) plan it
- (C) build it

4. You test a toy you made. It does not work. What should you do first?

- (A) retest it
- (B) rebuild it
- (C) redesign it

Engineering Design Process

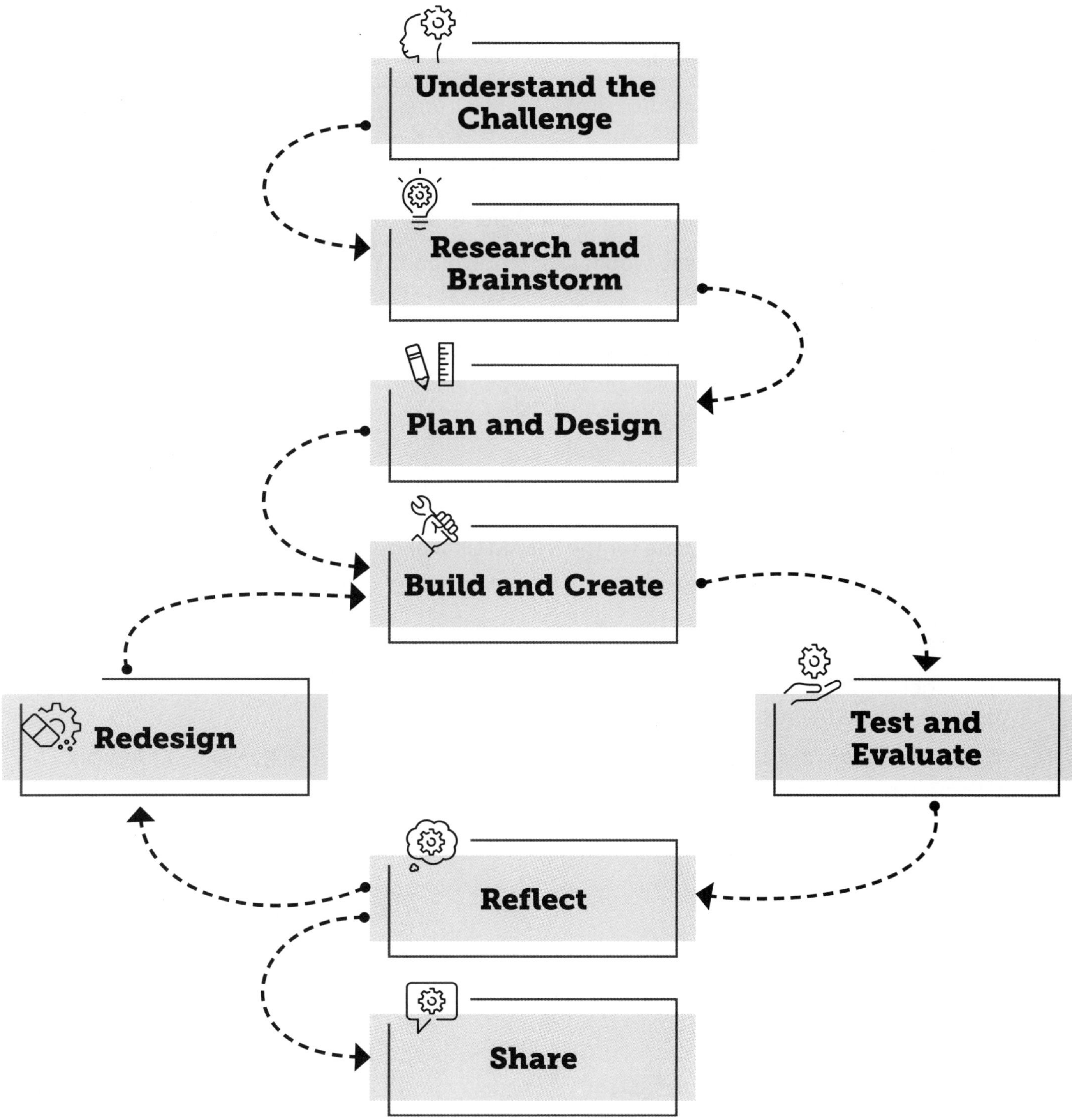

Digital Resources

Accessing the Digital Resources

The digital resources can be downloaded by following these steps:

1. Go to **www.tcmpub.com/digital**.
2. Use the ISBN number to redeem the digital resources.
3. Respond to the question using the book.
4. Follow the prompts on the Content Cloud website to sign in or create a new account.
5. Choose the digital resources you would like to download. You can download all the files at once or a specific group of files.

978-1-4258-2527-0

Contents of the Digital Resources

- Safety Contract
- Sentence frames to help guide friendly student feedback
- Materials requests for students' families
- Student Glossary
- Instructions for building a car base for the STEAM Challenge in Unit 3
- Materials list for the whole book

References Cited

Bybee, Rodger W. 2013. The Case for STEM Education: Challenges and Opportunities. Arlington, VA: NSTA Press.

NGSS Lead States. 2013. "Next Generation Science Standards: For States, By States APPENDIX I—Engineering Design in the NGSS." Washington, DC.

